CW01597458

2005
Post-Budget Supplement

by
David Smailes FCA

LexisNexis®
Tolley

Members of the LexisNexis Group worldwide

United Kingdom	LexisNexis Butterworths, a Division of Reed Elsevier (UK) Ltd, Halsbury House, 35 Chancery Lane, London, WC2A 1EL, and RSH, 1–3 Baxter's Place, Leith Walk Edinburgh EH1 3AF
Argentina	LexisNexis Argentina, BUENOS AIRES
Australia	LexisNexis Butterworths, CHATSWOOD, New South Wales
Austria	LexisNexis Verlag ARD Orac GmbH & Co KG, VIENNA
Canada	LexisNexis Butterworths, MARKHAM, Ontario
Chile	LexisNexis Chile Ltda, SANTIAGO DE CHILE
Czech Republic	Nakladatelství Orac sro, PRAGUE
France	Editions du Juris-Classeur SA, PARIS
Germany	LexisNexis Deutschland GmbH, FRANKFURT and MUNSTER
Hong Kong	LexisNexis Butterworths, HONG KONG
Hungary	HVG-Orac, BUDAPEST
India	LexisNexis Butterworths, NEW DELHI
Italy	Giuffrè Editore, MILAN
Malaysia	Malayan Law Journal Sdn Bhd, KUALA LUMPUR
New Zealand	LexisNexis Butterworths, WELLINGTON
Poland	Wydawnictwo Prawnicze LexisNexis, WARSAW
Singapore	LexisNexis Butterworths, SINGAPORE
South Africa	LexisNexis Butterworths, Durban
Switzerland	Stämpfli Verlag AG, BERNE
USA	LexisNexis, DAYTON, Ohio

Published by LexisNexis Butterworths

A CIP Catalogue record for this book is available from the British Library.

ISBN 0 7545 2863 4

Printed and bound by in Great Britain by Hobbs the Printers Ltd, Totton, Hampshire

Visit LexisNexis Butterworths at www.lexisnexis.co.uk

About This Supplement

This Supplement to Tolley's Income Tax 2004/05 gives details of changes in the law and practice of UK income tax from 2 July 2004 to 15 March 2005. It lists the changes in the same order and under the same paragraph headings as the annual publication. Also included is a summary of the proposals made in the Chancellor's Budget on 16 March 2005.

Each time Tolley's Income Tax 2004/05 is used, reference should be made to the material contained in this Supplement. The *Contents* give a list of all the chapters and paragraphs which have been updated.

TOLLEY

Contents

This Supplement contains amendments to the chapters and paragraphs of Tolley's Income Tax 2004/05 as listed below.

Contents

Contents

1 Allowances and Tax Rates

1.14 **Personal allowance.** The personal allowance for 2005/06 is £4,895 (*SI 2004 No 3161*). The second table on page 11 is updated to include 2005/06 figures as follows (see Pre-Budget Report, 2 December 2004).

	Personal allowance		Income	Maximum income	
	65 to 74	75 or over	limit	65 to 74	75 or over
For 2005/06	£7,090	£7,220	£19,500	£23,890	£24,150

1.15 **Married couple's allowance.** The basic married couple's allowance for 2005/06 is £2,280 (*SI 2004 No 3161*). The first table on page 13 is updated to include 2005/06 figures as follows (see Pre-Budget Report, 2 December 2004).

	Married couple's allowance		Income	Maximum income	
	65 to 74	75 or over	limit	65 to 74	75 or over
For 2005/06	£5,905	£5,975	£19,500	£31,140	£31,540

The following paragraph is added at the end.

'From a date still to be determined, registered same-sex couples are to be treated in the same way as married couples for tax purposes (Pre-Budget Report, 2 December 2004).' See now the Budget Summary for further details; the operative date is 5 December 2005.

1.19 **Blind persons.** The blind person's allowance for 2005/06 is £1,610 (*SI 2004 No 3161*).

3 Anti-Avoidance

3.1 **Introduction.** The following are added to the list of cases in the first paragraph: *CIR v Scottish Provident Institution HL 2004, [2005] STC 15* and *Barclays Mercantile Business Finance Ltd v Mawson HL 2004, [2005] STC 1.*

3.8 **Transfer pricing.** Immediately before the paragraph at the top of page 42 beginning 'The actual provision confers', the following paragraph is added.

'With effect from 4 March 2005, *Finance Act 2005* will (i) extend transfer pricing rules, so that they apply where parties who collectively could control a business act together to finance that business; and (ii) apply transfer pricing rules to financing put in place up to six months before a control relationship exists (Revenue Press Release 4 March 2005). Debt financing provided under pre-existing contracts will not fall within (i) above until 1 April 2007 or, if earlier, from the time of any change to the contract. For more details of these extensions to the transfer pricing rules, see www.inlandrevenue.gov.uk/international/transferpricing.pdf'

3.18 **Annual payments for non-taxable consideration.** The first paragraph is replaced with the following.

'Any payment (whenever the liability to make it was incurred, but subject to exceptions as below) of an annuity or other annual payment charged with tax under SCHEDULE D, CASE III (72), not being interest, and made for a consideration which is *not wholly* included in the income for tax purposes of the person making the annual payment, shall be paid without deduction of tax and not allowed as a deduction from, or a charge on, his income for the purposes of income tax and corporation tax. (Certain admission rights in return for annual payments to charities are disregarded for this purpose — see 14.17(*b*) CHARITIES). With backdated effect for payments made after 1 December 2004, the scope of this rule is to be extended by *FA 2005* to encompass any annual payment made in consideration for the receipt of a dividend or the right to receive a dividend (Pre-Budget Report, 2 December 2004).'

3.23 **Benefits from pre-owned assets.** Immediately below the paragraph on page 61 beginning 'For the purposes of these provisions', the following text is added.

'As a means of providing an exemption for open-market equity release schemes, the following additional excluded transactions have been announced:

- a sale before 7 March 2005, on arm's length terms, of *part* of the vendor's interest in the property; and
- a sale on or after 7 March 2005, on arm's length terms, of part of the vendor's interest in the property for a consideration other than money or readily realisable assets.

These additions will be made by statutory instrument. (Ministerial Statement 7 March 2005).'

At the end of the section on page 62 headed 'The chargeable amount', the following paragraph is added.

'It has been announced that the regulations will prescribe 6 April in each tax year as being the date at which valuations are to be made (or, if later and where applicable, the date in the year on which the asset first becomes chargeable). Land and chattels are to be valued every five years, with the valuation arrived at for the first year being used for that year and each of the next four years. The prescribed rate of interest for chattels is to be the same as the official rate applied to cheap employee loans (see 75.20 SCHEDULE E—EMPLOYMENT INCOME), i.e. **5%** for 2005/06. (Ministerial Statement 7 March 2005).'

On page 63, under 'Transitional election to disapply these provisions', it is noted that *regulations* are to be made to eliminate a potential double IHT charge that could otherwise arise in certain limited circumstances where the election is made (per Ministerial Statement 8 March 2005).

At the end of the paragraph spanning pages 63, 64 (under the heading 'Intangible property comprised in a settlement'), the following is added.

'The prescribed rate of interest is to be the same as the official rate applied to cheap employee loans (see 75.20 SCHEDULE E—EMPLOYMENT INCOME), i.e. **5%** for 2005/06 (Ministerial Statement 7 March 2005).'

3.24 **Disclosure of tax avoidance schemes.** The coverage is rewritten as follows to include *regulations* and other information not available at 1 July 2004 and to incorporate changes to the law since that date.

'With effect on and after **1 August 2004**, *FA 2004* imposes obligations, as outlined below, on promoters of certain tax avoidance schemes, and in some cases on persons entering into transactions under such schemes, to disclose those schemes to the Inland Revenue. The primary legislation provides the framework for these disclosure rules, with the detail provided by regulations made by statutory instrument.

The *Tax Avoidance Schemes (Prescribed Descriptions of Arrangements) Regulations 2004* (*SI 2004 No 1863* as amended by *SI 2004 No 2429*) apply the disclosure rules initially to certain arrangements related to financial products and certain arrangements connected with employment (in both cases with the features described in those regulations) and limits the scope of the rules to income tax, corporation tax and capital gains tax advantages. These regulations include, inter alia, a premium fee and confidentiality test whereby arrangements are excluded from the rules if

- it might reasonably be expected that no promoter, and no person connected with a promoter, of arrangements that are the same as, or substantially similar to, the arrangements in question would be able to obtain a 'premium fee' for them, *and*
- the tax advantage expected to be obtained under the arrangements does not arise from any element of the arrangements (including the way in which they are structured) which, disregarding any duty of confidentiality owed to any person, a promoter might reasonably be expected to wish to keep confidential from other promoters.

For this purpose, a '*premium fee*' is a fee which is chargeable by virtue of any element of the arrangements from which the anticipated tax advantage arises and is a fee the amount of which is to a significant extent attributable to, or which is to any extent contingent upon the obtaining of, that tax advantage.

The *Tax Avoidance Schemes (Information) Regulations 2004 (SI 2004 No 1864* as amended by *SI 2004 No 2613)* set out the procedural rules for disclosure, dealing with the manner and timing of disclosure and the information to be provided.

The Revenue have published detailed guidance notes on the disclosure rules (see www.inlandrevenue.gov.uk/aiu/guidance.pdf). For independent guidance, see Tolley's Tax Digest (Issue 28, December 2004) 'Disclosure of Tax Avoidance Schemes' and/or TAXline Tax Practice (Supplement No 9) 'Disclosure of Direct Tax Avoidance Schemes' published by the ICAEW Tax Faculty. The legislation is policed by the Revenue's Avoidance Intelligence Unit; see www.inlandrevenue.gov.uk/aiu/index.htm which includes links to the legislation and the official guidance plus various forms to be used for making disclosures.

Although the law came into force on 1 August 2004, it effectively applies retrospectively from, as the case may be, 18 March 2004 or 23 April 2004; see below for details, and see under Transitional provisions for further exclusions.

Obligations of promoters. A 'promoter' must provide the Board with specified information on any 'notifiable proposal' within five business days after the '*relevant date*', i.e. the date on which he makes the proposal available for implementation by any person or, if earlier, the date he first becomes aware of any transaction forming part of arrangements implementing the proposal. (The five-day period is extended if the promoter intends to apply to the Revenue for clearance under certain specified statutory provisions — see *SI 2004 No 1864, reg* 5.) A person is a '*promoter*' in relation to a 'notifiable proposal' if, in the course of a 'relevant business', he is to any extent responsible for the design of the proposed arrangements or he makes the 'notifiable proposal' available for implementation by others. The *Tax Avoidance Schemes (Promoter and Prescribed Circumstances) Regulations 2004 (SI 2004 No 1865)* exclude from the definition of 'promoter' (i) a company providing taxation services to another company in the same 51% group and (ii) an employee of the promoter or of a person entering into the proposed arrangements, and they also prescribe various circumstances in which a person to some extent responsible for the design of proposed arrangements is not to be regarded as a promoter by virtue of that fact alone. A '*notifiable proposal*' is a proposal for arrangements which, if entered into, would be '*notifiable arrangements*', i.e. arrangements falling within any description prescribed by regulations (see above) which enable (or might be expected to enable) any person to obtain a tax advantage (as widely defined) and are such that the main benefit, or one of the main benefits, that might be expected from them is the obtaining of that advantage.

There is a separate requirement for a 'promoter' to provide the Board with specified information relating to notifiable arrangements (as above) and to do so within five business days after the date on which he first becomes aware of any transaction forming part of those arrangements; but this does not apply if the arrangements implement a proposal which has been notified as above. A person is a '*promoter*' in relation to notifiable arrangements if, by virtue of his having made the proposal available for implementation, he is a promoter in relation to a notifiable proposal (as above) which is implemented by those arrangements or if, in the course of a 'relevant business', he is to any extent responsible for the design of the arrangements or the organisation or management of the arrangements.

A '*relevant business*' is any trade, profession or business which involves the provision to other persons of taxation services or is carried on by a bank or a securities house. Where companies form a 51% group, anything done by one group company for the purposes of another company's relevant business is brought within the above disclosure requirements.

Where two or more persons are promoters in relation to the same proposal or arrangements, notification by one promoter discharges the obligations of the others. If a promoter has discharged his obligations in relation to a proposal or arrangements, he is not required to notify proposals or arrangements which are substantially the same as those already notified (whether or not they relate to the same parties).

The above obligations do not apply in the case of any notifiable proposal for which the relevant date (as above) fell before 18 March 2004, any notifiable arrangements which implement such a proposal or any notifiable arrangements which include a transaction entered into before that date (and see also below under Transitional provisions).

Obligation of person dealing with non-UK promoter. A person who enters into any transaction forming part of notifiable arrangements in relation to which there is a non-UK resident promoter (and no UK resident promoter) must himself provide the Board with specified information relating to those arrangements. He must do so within five business days after entering into the transaction. This obligation is discharged if a promoter makes disclosure of the notifiable proposal for the arrangements in question. It does not apply in relation to any notifiable arrangements which include a transaction entered into before 23 April 2004 (and see also below under Transitional provisions).

Obligation of parties to notifiable arrangements not involving a promoter. A person who enters into any transaction forming part of notifiable arrangements in respect of which neither he nor any other person in the UK has an obligation as above must himself provide the Board with specified information relating to those arrangements. This does not apply in relation to any notifiable arrangements which include a transaction entered into before 23 April 2004 (and see also below under Transitional provisions). He may make such disclosure at any time after the date of the transaction and before he is first required to quote a reference number for the arrangements (see below).

Reference numbers allocated to arrangements. Where a person has made a disclosure as above, the Board may allocate a reference number to the arrangements in question and must notify the number to that person within 30 days after the disclosure. A promoter who is providing services to a client in connection with notifiable arrangements must pass on to the client the reference number for those arrangements or for arrangements which are substantially the same as those arrangements. He must do so within 30 days after the date he first becomes aware of any transaction forming part of the arrangements or, if later, the date on which the reference number is notified to him by the Board.

A party to any notifiable arrangements giving rise to an income tax or capital gains tax advantage must quote the allocated reference number in his personal tax return for the year in which the number is notified to him (or, if earlier, the year in which the tax advantage is expected to arise) and in all subsequent returns until the advantage ceases to apply to him. He must also quote the tax year in which, or the date on which, the advantage is expected to arise. Comparable provisions apply for corporation tax. For arrangements connected with employment, the obligation falls on the employer to quote the reference number etc. in the annual return on form P35 for the appropriate tax year. Persons not required to file a tax return or, as the case may be, a P35 return must instead provide the Revenue with specified information no later than what would have been the filing date for such a return.

Penalties. The maximum penalty for failure to comply with any of the disclosure obligations above is £5,000 (such penalty to be determined by the Special Commissioners). In the case of continuing failure after such a penalty is imposed, there is a daily penalty of up to £600 per day. Penalties of the same level apply if a promoter fails in his duty to notify a reference number to a client.

A party to notifiable arrangements who fails to give the reference number as required (for example, by including it in his tax return) is liable to a penalty of £100 for each scheme (i.e. each set of notifiable arrangements) to which the failure relates. A second such failure within a period of 36 months gives rise to a penalty of £500 per scheme. A third or subsequent failure within 36 months gives rise to a penalty of £1,000 per scheme. The pre-existing penalty regime for incorrect tax returns is, however, disapplied in relation to any such failure.

Legal professional privilege. These provisions do not require the disclosure of privileged information, i.e. information with respect to which a claim to legal professional privilege (or Scottish equivalent) could be maintained in legal proceedings. *However*, after 13 October 2004, the obligation to disclose is simply transferred from the promoter to the client; this is achieved by treating a case in which the promoter claims the protection of legal professional privilege as a case involving notifiable arrangements not involving a promoter (for which see above). In these circumstances, the client must make disclosure within the period of five business days after entering into the transaction. (If that period would otherwise have ended before 19 November 2004, it is treated as having ended on that date instead.) Alternatively the client has the option of informing the promoter that he does not wish to maintain a claim to legal privilege, in which case the obligation is passed back to the promoter (www.inlandrevenue.gov.uk/aiu/suppguide.htm).

Transitional provisions. Wherever a period of five business days for making disclosure applies (see above) and that period would otherwise have ended before 30 September 2004, it is treated as having ended on that date instead (subject to the later date given above in cases involving legal professional privilege).

Arrangements involving *financial products* do not have to be disclosed if, as the case may be, the relevant date (see above under Obligations of Promoters), the date on which a promoter first became aware of a transaction or the date on which a transaction was entered into, fell before 22 June 2004. If the appropriate date fell on or after 22 June 2004 but before 1 August 2004, disclosure is required but can be made at any time before 1 November 2004.

In the case of arrangements involving *employment products*, if, as the case may be, the relevant date, the date on which a promoter first became aware of a transaction or the date on which a transaction was entered into, fell before 1 August 2004, disclosure is required but can be made at any time before 1 November 2004.

[*TMA 1970, s 98C; FA 2004, ss 306–319; SI 2004 Nos 1863, 1864, 1865, 2429, 2613*].

Simon's Direct Tax Service. See A3.19.'

4 Appeals

4.17 **Hearing and determination of proceedings.** In the paragraph on page 80 beginning '*Orders for costs*', *Jones v Garnett (Sp C 432), [2005] SSCD 9* and *Carvill v Frost (Sp C 447), [2005] SSCD 208* are added to the list of cases in which costs were awarded to the taxpayer, and *Conlon v Hewitt (Sp C 436), [2005] SSCD 46* is added to the list of cases in which the taxpayer applied for costs and was refused.

5 Assessments

5.3 **Further assessments on 'discovery'.** The coverage of the important case of *Langham v Veltema* is expanded to read as follows.

'The categories in (i)–(iv) above constitute an exhaustive definition of 'information made available to an officer of the Board' for the purpose of (2)(*b*) above; an officer is not precluded from making a discovery assessment simply because some other information (not normally part of the officer's immediate checks) might be available (in the instant case a form P11D) that might place doubt on the sufficiency of the self-assessment (*Langham v Veltema CA, [2004] STC 544*). Following this important CA decision, the Revenue produced a guidance note in December 2004 (see www.inlandrevenue.gov.uk/news/veltema_guide_note.pdf). In particular, a taxpayer can protect himself from a discovery assessment by stating (truthfully) in his tax return

- (in cases involving valuations) that a valuation has been used and that it was carried out by a named independent and suitably qualified valuer on an appropriate basis (but such protection is not available in the circumstances present in *Langham v Veltema*, i.e. where the same transaction is the subject of an agreed valuation in a tax return made by another party to the transaction);
- (in cases involving other judgmental issues, for example where expenditure on property is allocated between non-deductible capital expenditure, e.g. improvements to property, and deductible revenue expenditure, e.g. repairs) that a programme of work has been carried out and the expenditure allocated on a particular basis; and
- (where such is the case) that a view of the law has been taken which differs from a published view taken by the Revenue.

In no case does the taxpayer need to supply sufficient information to *quantify* a possible insufficiency in the self-assessment; the object of the exercise is merely to draw the Revenue's attention to the possible existence of such insufficiency.'

9 Capital Allowances

9.4A **Business Premises Renovation Allowance (BPRA).** A new paragraph is added as follows.

'Subject to consultation and receipt of EU State Aid approval, a 100% first-year allowance is to be introduced for capital expenditure incurred by individuals and companies (whether as landlords or tenants) on the renovation or conversion of vacant business premises in any of the disadvantaged areas of the UK designated as 'Enterprise Areas' for the purposes of bringing those premises back into business use. It is suggested that the allowances be restricted to property that has remained unused for at least 12 months, but this itself is subject to consultation. Although the legislation is expected in 2005, the effective commencement date is as yet undetermined. The scheme will run for 5 years from date of introduction. (Pre-Budget Report, 2 December 2004).'

9.24 **Plant and machinery: qualifying expenditure and activities.** The case citation in the first paragraph is updated to read: *Barclays Mercantile Business Finance Ltd v Mawson HL 2004, [2005] STC 1.*

Item (vi) in the list of qualifying activities spanning pages 147, 148 is amended to read: 'managing the investments of a company with investment business'. This change applies from, broadly, 1 April 2004 and is made by *SI 2004 No 2310, Sch paras 52, 53.*

The following paragraph is added at the end.

'**Proposed reform of rules on leasing of plant and machinery.** Subject to consultation, the rules on leasing of plant and machinery are to be reformed in *FA 2006*, draft legislation having been published as part of the 2004 Pre-Budget Report. For finance leases, the new regime will give capital allowances to the lessee rather than to the lessor as at present. There will be corresponding changes to the tax treatment of lease rentals, to ensure that the lessor is no longer taxed on, and the lessee does not obtain a deduction for, the capital element of rentals. The new regime will apply only to leases which are essentially financing transactions, to be known as '*funding leases*', comprising mainly finance leases but also a small proportion of operating leases. Short leases (possibly to be defined as those not exceeding four years) will be excluded from the regime. Pre-existing leases are unlikely to be affected. (Pre-Budget Report, 2 December 2004).'

9.25 **Plant and machinery: eligible expenditure.** The final case citation on page 149 is updated to read: *Anchor International Ltd v CIR CS, 2004 STI 2298.*

9.27 **Plant and machinery: first-year allowances.** In the definition of 'energy-saving plant or machinery' spanning pages 159, 160, it is noted that, with effect after 25 August 2004, air-to-air energy recovery equipment, compact heat exchangers and heating, ventilation and air conditioning zone controls are added to the Energy Technology Product List (*SI 2004 No 2093*).

In the definition of 'environmentally beneficial plant or machinery' spanning pages 160, 161, it is noted that, with effect after 25 August 2004, rainwater harvesting equipment is added to the Water Technology Product List (*SI 2004 No 2094*).

9.35 **Plant and machinery: overseas leasing.** After the fourth paragraph on page 193 (beginning 'Where there is a chain of leases'), the following paragraph is added.

'The Revenue continued to be of the opinion that in determining whether or not overseas leasing is 'protected leasing' (see (*a*) and (*e*) below), it was necessary to consider only the end lease in a chain. They now take the view that every lease in the chain must be considered; if the leasing under any of the leases is not 'protected leasing', the overseas leasing restrictions apply to the whole chain. The Revenue will apply their earlier view to leasing arrangements entered into before 3 February 2005, or within three months after that date where the principal terms were agreed in writing before that date and did not materially alter in the intervening period. (Revenue Internet Statement 3 February 2005).'

13 Certificates of Tax Deposit

13.2 The following entry is added to the list of rates for deposits of less than £100,000.

	Used to pay tax	Withdrawals for cash
6 August 2004 onwards	1.25%	0.5%

13.3 The following entry is added to the list of rates for deposits of £100,000 or more used to meet a scheduled liability.

	Period of deposit in months				
	Under 1	1 but under 3	3 but under 6	6 but under 9	9 but under 12
6 August 2004 onwards	1.25%	3.75%	3.75%	3.75%	3.75%

14 Charities

At the beginning of the chapter, a new cross-reference is inserted as follows:

'See 'A guide to tax incentives for corporate giving', published jointly by the Treasury and Home Office (and available at www.inlandrevenue.gov.uk/charities/guide_tax_incentives.pdf), which, despite its title, covers charitable giving by all businesses and not just by companies.'

14.14 **Gift Aid: limits on donor benefits.** The first paragraph on page 251 is expanded to read as follows.

'In applying the above limits, the benefit of a right of free or reduced-price admission for the donor or a member of his family

(A) to view property, the preservation of which for the public benefit is the sole or main purpose of the charity; or

(B) to observe wildlife, the conservation of which for the public benefit is the sole or main purpose of the charity;

is disregarded provided that the opportunity to make gifts which attract such a right is available to members of the public. For the wider application in practice of this relief, see para 3.48 of the Revenue guide referred to at 14.11 above. From April 2006, these disregards will be widened to allow more types of charity to benefit and will be amended to embrace donations of at least 10% more than the normal admission charge and donations resulting in unlimited admission rights for a period of at least twelve months (Pre-Budget Report, 2 December 2004, para 5.80).'

14.18 **Payroll Giving Schemes.** At the end, the following new paragraph is added.

'**Payroll Giving Grants.** Businesses with 500 employees or less which set up a payroll giving scheme between 6 April 2004 and 31 December 2006 may be entitled to a Government grant of up to £500. In addition (until the scheme ends in March 2007), the first £10 per month of each employees' donations for the first six months (from the time the employee commences payroll giving) will be matched by Government donation to the charities in question. For more details, see www.payrollgivinggrants.org.uk'

18 Compensation for Loss of Employment (and Damages)

18.3 **Compensation for termination of office or employment (general tax law).** In the first full paragraph on page 284, the following is added immediately before the final sentence:

'But voluntary payments of £30,000 each made to the former directors of a family company the day after their resignation and retirement and minuted as being 'in appreciation of [their] services to the company over many years' were held by a Special Commissioner to be for services rendered and chargeable to tax as general earnings (*Allum and another v Marsh (Sp C 446), [2005] SSCD 191*.'

20 Construction Industry Scheme (CIS)

20.2 **Payments from which tax must be deducted.** Before the paragraph on page 294 beginning 'Private householders', the following paragraph is added.

'The fact that a person's construction operations may not be part of his core business or may not be substantive does not prevent his being a contractor for the purposes of these provisions (*Mundial Invest SA v Moore Ch D, 2005 STI 278*).'

20.4 **Subcontractors' tax certificates.** In the paragraph beginning 'An *individual applicant*' spanning pages 297, 298, *Arnold v G-Con Ltd Ch D, 2005 STI 364* is added to the case already cited.

23 Diplomatic etc. Immunity—Individuals and Organisations

23.1 After the first paragraph, the following paragraph is added.

'In *Jimenez v CIR (Sp C 419), [2004] SSCD 371*, a person employed as a cook by the Namibian High Commission in London was denied income tax exemption on her earnings, otherwise available under *Diplomatic Privileges Act 1964* and *article 37(3)* of the *Vienna Convention on Diplomatic Relations* (which provides exemption for 'members of the service staff' of a diplomatic mission who are not 'permanently resident in the receiving State'), because she had not been notified to the UK authorities as a member of a diplomatic mission in the UK.'

24 Double Tax Relief

24.2 **Double tax agreements.** The UK/Georgia agreement (*SI 2004 No 3325*) is added to the list, though it is noted that this is not yet in force. It is noted that the UK/New Zealand protocol (*SI 2004 No 1274*) applies from *broadly* 6 April 2005 (UK) and 1 April 2005 (New Zealand) — per Revenue Press Release 17 August 2004.

The first of the Notes below the list of agreements is updated to read as follows.

'*Agreements not yet in force.* The above-mentioned Agreement with Belarus had not yet entered into force at 1 August 2004. (Revenue Tax Bulletin August 2004 p 1140).'

The last of the Notes is updated to read as follows.

'*Yugoslavia.* The Agreement published as *SI 1981 No 1815* between the UK and Yugoslavia is regarded as remaining in force between the UK and, respectively, Bosnia-Herzegovina, Croatia, Macedonia, Serbia and Montenegro, and Slovenia. (Revenue Statement of Practice SP 03/04, 28 September 2004 (replacing SP 6/93)).'

24.9 **EU Savings Directive — special withholding tax.** It is noted that the EU Savings Directive is now due to come into force on 1 July 2005.

25 Enterprise Investment Scheme

25.2 **Conditions for relief.** At the end of the para spanning pages 356, 357 and beginning 'Paragraph (*b*) above may be satisfied', the following is added:

'Paragraph (*b*) was held to be satisfied where the money raised was loaned to overseas subsidiaries for the purpose of enabling them to supply information and analysis for the purposes of the issuing company's business (*4 Cast Ltd v Mitchell (Sp C 455), 2005 STI 162*).'

28 Exempt Income

28.3 **Child Trust Funds.** A number of changes has been made to the text, which now reads as follows.

'Broadly, there is no tax on the income or gains of a Child Trust Fund (see below for more details). Similarly, there will be no tax charges when the fund matures on the child's 18th birthday.

The Child Trust Fund (CTF) was established in order to provide all children with a financial asset at the start of adult life, to encourage savings and investment, and to help people to engage with financial institutions. Given these aims, it is not surprising that the legislation detailing the characteristics of an account that may qualify as a CTF, and those who may provide such accounts, is carefully drawn to protect the assets until the child reaches 18.

An account with an approved provider may be opened in respect of a child born after 31 August 2002 where (broadly) there is an entitlement to child benefit (an 'eligible child'). CTFs become fully operational on 6 April 2005, but it is possible to go through the formalities of opening an account at any time on or after 1 January 2005.

The process of opening an account begins with the Revenue issuing a voucher to the person who is entitled to child benefit in respect of an eligible child. The voucher must be given to an account provider within twelve months of issue. There is provision to appeal against a Revenue decision not to issue such a voucher.

An account may be opened by a responsible person (broadly, a person with parental responsibility) or (looking forward to September 2018 and beyond) by an eligible child who is over 16. If there is no responsible person, or if a voucher has been issued but not given to an account provider within twelve months, the Revenue will open an account. At any time only a single responsible person, or only the child if over 16, is able to give instructions to the account provider as to the management of the account. This person is designated the 'registered contact'. There is provision for the Official Solicitor (in Scotland, the Accountant of Court) to manage the CTF accounts of looked after children for whom nobody (or nobody suitable) has parental responsibility.

In truth, the decisions to be made about the management of the account are limited. However, it is possible to swap to another account provider (at the cost only of incidental expenses) or to swap to an account of another description or type offered by the same account provider (once again, at the cost only of incidental expenses).

Accounts may be of two types: stakeholder accounts and non-stakeholder accounts. Stakeholder accounts are subject to stringent rules about the charges that may be deducted from them, and have a more restricted range of permissible investments and investment strategies (see below). Certain accounts, chiefly those opened by the Revenue, have to be stakeholder accounts.

Contributions to the account. The Revenue will make an initial payment into the account. The amount of this initial contribution is £250 (£500 for children in care), but there are small increases to this figure for eligible children born before 6 April 2005. The initial contribution is supplemented by a further £250 if (broadly) child tax credit is payable at the time child benefit is first paid and either (i) income is below the threshold for child tax credit (see 83.7 SOCIAL SECURITY) or (ii) income support or income-based job-seekers' allowance is being claimed. The amount of the supplementary payment is subject to small increases where child benefit was first paid prior to 6 April 2005.

A top-up payment will be made by the Revenue to the account when the child reaches the age of seven. Subject to consultation on the amounts, this may again be £250, once more doubled to £500 in the case of children in lower income families — judged at the child's seventh birthday. (Pre-Budget Report, 2 December 2004).

There is provision for the Revenue to recoup their contributions where the account is invalid and cannot be 'repaired' (see under Administration below) or where the basis for the supplementary contribution is removed because of a change in the tax credit/benefit position. Any decision not to pay a contribution, or to recoup contributions, is subject to a right of appeal.

In addition to these government payments, anyone, including the child, may pay into the account. However, there is a limit of £1,200 for such contributions in any one year. A 'year' for this purpose is the period from the opening of the account to the child's next birthday, and each succeeding period of twelve months. If the limit is not reached in any year, it is not possible to carry forward the unused part. Neither is there any provision for a carry-back of contributions.

Only monetary payments may be accepted, so there is no possibility of gifting shares or other assets into a CTF.

Withdrawals from the account. Withdrawals from the account are not permitted before the child reaches the age of 18. There are three exceptions to this. The first is that the account provider is allowed to make deductions in respect of management charges and incidental expenses. The second is where the child is terminally ill. The third is where the child dies before reaching 18.

The investments under a CTF are inalienable — any charge over them, or assignment of them is void. If the child is made bankrupt, creditors may not gain access to the account.

Qualifying investments. There are extensive strictures regarding permitted investments for a CTF account. In order to help account providers, the structure of the regulations governing CTF accounts has been modelled on the provisions relating to Individual Savings Accounts. Qualifying investments for CTFs are as follows.

(*a*) Shares issued by a company (other than an investment trust, but see (*e*) below) wherever incorporated, and officially listed on a recognised stock exchange. There are rules to allow the official listing condition to be treated as satisfied in the case of shares issued under a public offer and due to be listed. However, shares do not qualify if they have been acquired on favourable terms because of a connection with the allocation or allotment of other shares, securities or rights thereto.

(*b*) Securities issued by a company wherever incorporated, provided either the securities themselves, or the shares in the issuing company, or the shares in a parent company (of which the issuing company is a 75% subsidiary) are officially listed on a recognised stock exchange. In the case of securities in an investment trust, the investment trust must have no 'eligible rental income' (see Tolley's Corporation Tax under Unit and Investment Trusts).

(*c*) Gilt-edged securities.

(*d*) Securities issued by or on behalf of a government of any EEA State, and strips of such securities.

(*e*) Shares in an investment trust listed in the Official List of the Stock Exchange. Broadly, in order to qualify, an investment trust must have no 'eligible rental income' (see Tolley's Corporation Tax under Unit and Investment Trusts).

(*f*) Units in, or shares of, a securities scheme, warrant scheme or fund of funds scheme.

(*g*) Units in, or shares of, a money-market scheme.

(*h*) Units in, or shares of, a UCITS (Undertaking for Collective Investment in Transferable Securities).

(*j*) A depositary interest.

(*k*) Cash deposited in a share or deposit account with a building society or deposit account with a bank (as defined in *ICTA 1988, s 840A(1)(b)*) or a relevant European institution. However, a deposit or share account is not a qualifying investment if it is 'connected' with any other investment. For this purpose, an account is '*connected*' with another investment if either was opened or acquired with reference to the other, or with a view to enabling the other to be opened or acquired on particular terms, or with a view to facilitating the opening or acquisition of the other on particular terms *and* the terms on which the account was opened would have been significantly less favourable to the holder if the investment had not been acquired.

(*l*) Designated national savings products.

(*m*) Life insurance policies satisfying specified conditions (see below).

In order to qualify, a life insurance policy must insure the life of the child only. Its terms and conditions must provide:

- that the policy may only be owned or held as a qualifying investment for a CTF account;
- that the policy will terminate if it comes to the notice of the account provider that there has been a breach of the CTF regulations relating to insurance policies, and the breach cannot be remedied as a repair to an invalid account (see below under Administration);

- for the express prohibition of payments resulting from termination or partial surrender to the child before age 18;
- that the policy etc. cannot be assigned other than by transfer of title between approved account providers or by its vesting in the child's personal representatives.

The contract of insurance must either fall within the *Financial Services and Markets Act 2000 (Regulated Activities) Order 2001, Sch 1 Pt 2* (contract of long-term insurance), *para 1* (life insurance) or *para 3* (life insurance where benefits linked to value of property), or be capable of falling within either of those paragraphs were the insurer to be a company with permission under *Financial Services and Markets Act 2000* to effect insurance contracts.

The policy must constitute life insurance and must not be a contract to pay a life annuity, a personal portfolio bond (see 45.13 LIFE ASSURANCE POLICIES) or a contract constituting pension business (as defined). There must be no contractual obligation to pay any premium other than the first (so regular premium policies are excluded). The making of loans by, or by arrangement with, the insurer to, or at the direction of, the child or registered contact is prohibited.

Stakeholder accounts. There are further restrictions on investment, and investment strategy, for stakeholder accounts. Broadly, they must not invest directly in shares, investment trusts or certain types of insurance contract. Investment in securities, authorised unit trusts and open-ended investment companies is subject to specific conditions. Interest must accrue at a specified minimum rate (linked to base rate) in respect of cash held in deposit or share accounts. As regards investment strategy, there is a requirement for the account to be exposed to equities. The account provider must have regard to the need for diversification, and must consider investment options in the light of the purpose of the account. For the last five years or so of the account, the account provider must consider the need to minimise fluctuations in the capital value of the account resulting from market conditions.

Tax treatment. No tax is chargeable in respect of interest, dividends, distributions or gains on account investments. (For capital gains tax purposes, assets in the fund are treated as sold and immediately re-acquired at market value just prior to the child's 18th birthday.) To maintain symmetry, capital gains tax losses on account investments are disregarded. Any income from account investments is not to be regarded as income for any income tax purposes — this exemption specifically embraces the children's settlements provisions at 81.18 SETTLEMENTS.

There are, in addition, disapplications of provisions taxing profits or gains under the accrued income scheme (see 74.5 SCHEDULE D, CASE VI), offshore income gains (see 52 OFFSHORE FUNDS), and discounts on relevant discounted securities (see 72.5 SCHEDULE D, CASE III). Life assurance gains (see 45.13 LIFE ASSURANCE POLICIES) are not taxable (and a deficiency on termination is not deductible from the child's total income) provided regulatory conditions are not breached (see below). Companies and local authorities may pay interest etc. gross.

It is up to the account provider to make tax claims, conduct appeals, and agree liabilities and reliefs on behalf of the child or registered contact. It is unlikely then that the child or registered contact will have to deal with any tax matters arising from the account. However, there is power for the Board to make an assessment under Schedule D, Case VI on the registered contact as an alternative to the account provider in order to withdraw relief or recover tax. This is subject to the right of appeal.

Where a life assurance policy becomes invalid because of a breach of the regulations (see above under Qualifying investments*)* a chargeable event then occurs. That event, and any prior chargeable event becomes taxable under the normal provisions relating to life assurance gains (see 45.13 *et seq.* LIFE ASSURANCE POLICIES). Lower rate tax is payable by the account provider (with the Revenue having the power to tax the registered contact). Any higher rate tax due is payable by the registered contact by assessment within five years after 31 January following the year in which the chargeable event or termination occurred.

Administration. Administration of the account largely rests with the account provider. Regulations cover: qualification as an account manager; Revenue approval and withdrawal thereof (and appeals against these decisions); appointment of UK tax representatives of non-UK account managers; account managers ceasing to act or qualify; transfer of accounts to other account providers; annual and fortnightly electronic returns of information; annual and interim tax repayment claims; record-keeping; and information to be provided to the named child (including annual statements).

The account provider and the registered contact are required to take any necessary steps to remedy any breach of the regulations surrounding the CTF account. Provided this is done the account remains valid during the period of the breach, although penalties may still be in point. There are, however, two breaches where no repair is possible:

- where the child has never been an eligible child; and
- where more than one account is held for the same child.

In the above circumstances, Revenue contributions, plus any consequent income and gains, will be recouped, the account provider, registered contact and named child being jointly and severally liable.

The Revenue have wide powers to require information and to inspect records in relation to CTF accounts. This is subject to a penalty regime analogous to that for special returns in *TMA 1970, s 98* (see 57.9 PENALTIES).

There is a penalty of up to £300 for fraudulently opening, or making a withdrawal from, a CTF account.

[*Child Trust Funds Act 2004; SI 2004 Nos 1450, 2422, 2676, 3369, 3382; SI 2005 No 383*].

'*SI 2005 No 340* and *No 341* (amending, respectively, *SI 1994 No 1812* and *SI 1994 No 1811* — see 4.7 APPEALS) enable the General and Special Commissioners to hear CTF appeals against Inland Revenue decisions. *SI 2005 No 191* makes separate provision for non-tax CTF appeals.'

For practical guidance, see the Child Trust Fund website at www.childtrustfund.gov.uk See also the Revenue's guidance for account providers at www.inlandrevenue.gov.uk/ctf/ctfguidancenotes.pdf'

28.6 **Damages and compensation for personal injury — periodical payments.** The final paragraph is updated to read as follows.

'The above provisions apply equally to annuity payments under a compensation award under the Criminal Injuries Compensation Scheme. The Treasury may also apply them (with any necessary modifications) to any other scheme or arrangement making similar provision. After 4 August 2004, the provisions are thus applied to recipients of payments from the Thalidomide Children's Trust established on 10 August 1973 (*SI 2004 No 1819*).'

28.13 **Individual Savings Accounts.** A number of changes have been made to the text, which now reads as follows.

'**For 1998/99 onwards**, individuals aged 18 or over (reduced to 16 from 6 April 2001 in the case of cash only accounts (as below)) who are resident and ordinarily resident in the UK are able to subscribe up to £7,000 in each tax year to an individual savings account (an ISA) set up in accordance with regulations. Before 2005/06, the account may contain three components: cash (including National Savings); life insurance; and stocks and shares. Of the annual subscription, no more than £3,000 may go into cash and £1,000 into life insurance. For 2005/06 onwards, the life insurance component is abolished. Shares acquired under approved profit-sharing or SAYE option schemes or share incentive plans (see 82.18, 82.47, 82.20 SHARE-RELATED EMPLOYMENT INCOME AND EXEMPTIONS) may be transferred in at market value (with no capital gains tax liability) within the annual subscription limits, but public offer and demutualisation issues may not be transferred in. Life insurance products have to be of the single premium type (i.e. there must be no obligation to keep up premium payments in order to obtain policy benefits), although policies with recurrent single premiums or regular monthly premiums are acceptable. There is no minimum subscription, no lifetime limit and no loss of relief on withdrawals. It is guaranteed that the arrangements will continue for at least ten years.

The £7,000 and £3,000 limits above were to be reduced (to £5,000 and £1,000 respectively) for 2006/07 onwards but, subject to consultation, are now to be extended so as to apply to all years up to and including 2008/09 (Pre-Budget Report, 2 December 2004).

Personal equity plans (see 28.24 below) held at 5 April 1999 may continue to be held without affecting the ability to invest in an individual savings account. Similarly, investments in TESSAs started before 6 April 1999 did not affect individual savings account investments, and the capital (but *not* the accrued interest) in a maturing TESSA could be transferred to an individual savings account in addition to the normal investment limits.

There is an exemption from income tax and capital gains tax on the investments, and for the first five years for which the accounts are available (i.e. until 5 April 2004), *FA 1998, s 76* disapplied the rule introduced by *F(No 2)A 1997, s 30* preventing payment of the tax credit attached to UK dividends (see 1.9 ALLOWANCES AND TAX RATES), so that the 10% tax credit was payable (and regulations make similar provision in respect of non-resident holders of accounts —see below). Similar provision was made in relation to insurance company and friendly society investments referable to individual savings account business.

The necessary regulation-making powers are provided in general by amendment to the personal equity plan regulations [*FA 1998, s 75*], and in relation to life insurance investments and FRIENDLY SOCIETIES (31) by *FA 1998, s 77*. Accounts, which must be administered by managers, may be offered by financial institutions or by independent providers. Managers will be able to offer accounts either accepting overall subscriptions (which must be able to accept the annual maximum, and so *must* offer a stocks and shares component and *may* offer either or both of the other two components) or accepting one of the three components (within the applicable annual maximum, including a £4,000 maximum (£3,000 before 2005/06) in relation to a stocks and shares account). The life assurance component is abolished for 2005/06 onwards.

The Individual Savings Account Regulations 1998 (*SI 1998 No 1870* as amended) provide for the setting up by Revenue-approved accounts managers of plans in the form of an account (an ISA) under which individuals may make certain investments, for the conditions under which they may invest and under which the accounts are to operate, for relief from tax in respect of account investments, and for general administration.

General. An application to subscribe to an ISA may be made by an individual who is 18 or over (16 or over from 6 April 2001 in the case of cash only accounts) and who is resident and ordinarily resident in the UK (or is a non-UK resident Crown employee whose duties are in effect treated as performed in the UK, see 75.4 SCHEDULE E—EMPLOYMENT INCOME, or, from 6 April 2001, the spouse of such an employee). Joint accounts are not permitted. An investor who subsequently fails to meet the residence requirement may retain the account and the right to tax exemptions thereunder but can make no further subscriptions to the account until he again comes to meet that requirement. After 7 January 2003, an application made on behalf of an individual suffering from mental disorder, by a parent, guardian, spouse, son or daughter of his, is treated as if made by that individual. This replaced a rule specific to Scotland whereby a *curator bonis* appointed in respect of a qualifying individual incapable of managing his affairs could subscribe to an ISA in his capacity as such without affecting his right to subscribe in any other capacity.

An ISA is made up of *one or more* of the following: a stocks and shares component, a cash component and (before 2005/06) an insurance component (see below re qualifying investments for each of these components). It must be designated from the outset as a maxi-account, mini-account or TESSA only account, such designation continuing to have effect for any year in which the investor makes a subscription to the account.

A *maxi-account* must comprise a stocks and shares component (*with or without* other components). The maximum subscription per tax year is £7,000 of which a maximum of £3,000 may be allocated to a cash component and £1,000 (for 2004/05 and earlier years) to an insurance component. For 2001/02 and subsequent years, where the subscriber is 16 but under 18 at the end of the tax year, the limit is lowered to £3,000, which may only be invested in a cash component, and in the year in which the subscriber attains the age of 18 that limit and restriction apply to subscriptions before his or her birthday. In any tax year in which an investor subscribes to a maxi-account he cannot subscribe to any other ISA apart from a TESSA only account.

A *mini-account* must consist of a single specified component. The maximum subscription (per tax year) is £4,000 (£3,000 before 2005/06) if that component is stocks and shares, £1,000 if it is insurance (applicable only to 2004/05 and earlier years) and £3,000 if it is cash. In any tax year in which an investor subscribes to a mini-account, he cannot subscribe to another mini-account consisting of the same component or to a maxi-account.

A *TESSA only account* is an account consisting of a cash component only and limited to capital (*not* accumulated interest) transferred from a TESSA (see 28.16(iii) below) within six months following its maturity after 5 April 1999 (or after 5 January 1999 where no follow-up TESSA is opened). Such transfers are not subject to any annual subscription limit, and may also be made to a maxi-account or to a cash component mini-account without counting towards the annual subscription limits for such accounts.

Subscriptions to an ISA must be made in cash (and must be allocated irrevocably to the agreed component or single component) *except that* shares acquired by the investor under a SAYE option scheme (see 82.47 SHARE-RELATED EMPLOYMENT INCOME AND EXEMPTIONS) or a share incentive plan (see 82.20 SHARE-RELATED EMPLOYMENT INCOME AND EXEMPTIONS) or appropriated to him under an approved profit sharing scheme (see 82.18 SHARE-RELATED EMPLOYMENT INCOME AND EXEMPTIONS) may be transferred to a stocks and shares component. Such transfers count towards the annual subscription limits, by reference to the market value of the shares at the date of transfer. No chargeable gain or allowable loss arises on the transfer. A transfer of SAYE scheme shares must be made within 90 days after the exercise of the option, and a transfer of share incentive plan shares must be made within 90 days of the shares ceasing to be subject to the plan. A transfer of shares appropriated under a profit sharing scheme must be made within 90 days after the earlier of the release date (see 82.19 SHARE-RELATED EMPLOYMENT INCOME AND EXEMPTIONS) and the date on which the investor instructed the scheme trustees to transfer ownership of the shares to him. From 13 December 2000, 'shares' in these cases includes a reference to those held in the form of depositary interests (see (*j*) below).

Compensation paid into ISAs for loss of income or capital growth due to failures or delays on the part of ISA managers will not count towards the subscription limit. This does not apply to compensation paid in respect of a delay in opening an ISA, or in accepting a subscription to an ISA. See Revenue Guidance Notes for ISA Managers paras 10.38, 10.39 and PEP and ISA Bulletin 4, 13 December 2001.

ISA investments cannot be purchased otherwise than out of cash held by the account manager and allocated to the particular component concerned, and cannot be purchased from the investor or the investor's spouse.

The title to ISA investments (other than cash deposits, national savings products and certain insurance policies) is vested in the account manager (or his nominee) either alone or jointly with the investor, though all ISA investments are in the beneficial ownership of the investor.

The investor may elect to receive annual reports and accounts etc. in respect of ISA investments and/or to attend and vote at shareholders' etc. meetings.

The statements and declarations to be made when applying to subscribe to an ISA are specified. The maximum penalty for an incorrect statement or declaration is the amount (if any) of income tax and/or capital gains tax underpaid as a result. Assessments to withdraw tax relief or otherwise recover tax underpaid may be made (under SCHEDULE D, CASE VI (74) in the case of income tax) on the account manager or investor. The Revenue have power to require information from, and to inspect records of, account managers and investors.

From 1 October 2002 (and with reference to pre-existing ISAs as well as new ones), the terms and conditions of an ISA cannot prevent the investor from withdrawing funds or from transferring his account (or a part of it) to another Revenue-approved account manager (subject to the conditions governing such transfers). The account manager is allowed a reasonable business period (not exceeding 30 days) to comply with the investor's instructions in this regard. By concession, an ISA opened before 24 August 2002 offering a fixed or guaranteed return under terms requiring the funds to be locked in for a period of up to five years may, if the manager wishes and with Revenue agreement, continue to maturity under its original terms, though no further subscriptions can be made after 5 April 2003. (Revenue Press Release 26 July 2002).

Tax exemptions. Except as stated below, no income tax or capital gains tax is chargeable on the account manager or the investor in respect of interest, dividends, distributions or gains on ISA investments. Capital losses are not allowable. As stated in the introduction above, tax credits on UK dividends paid before 6 April 2004 are repayable (via the account manager). An investor who ceases to be UK-resident is treated as continuing to be so resident as regards his entitlement to repayment of tax credits.

Interest on a cash deposit held within a stocks and shares component or (before 2005/06) an insurance component is, however, taxable at the lower rate of income tax, such tax to be accounted for by the account manager (by set-off against tax repayments or otherwise). There is no further liability; the interest does not form part of the investor's total income and the tax paid cannot be repaid to the investor.

Life assurance gains on policies held within an ISA are not subject to income tax (and a deficiency on termination is not deductible from the investor's total income). If it comes to the account manager's notice that such a policy is invalid, i.e. its terms and conditions do not provide (or no longer provide) that it be held only as a qualifying insurance component investment, a chargeable event then occurs, with any gain taxable under SCHEDULE D, CASE VI (74). If the policy has already terminated, the chargeable event is deemed to have occurred at the end of the final policy year (see 45.15(*a*) LIFE ASSURANCE POLICIES). Any previous chargeable event which actually occurred in relation to the policy is similarly taxed, by reference to the time it occurred. Lower rate income tax (for 2005/06 onwards, previously basic rate income tax) is payable by the account manager (with the Revenue also having power to assess the investor). Any higher rate tax due is payable by the investor by assessment within five years after 31 January following the year of assessment in which the chargeable event occurred or was deemed to occur. Top-slicing relief (see 45.13 LIFE ASSURANCE POLICIES) is available in the same way as for non-ISA-related chargeable events.

Exempt income and gains do not have to be reported in the investor's personal tax return.

Further capital gains matters. A transfer of ISA investments by an account manager to an investor is deemed to be made at market value, with no capital gain or allowable loss arising. An investor is treated as holding shares or securities in an ISA in a capacity other than that in which he holds any other shares etc. of the same class in the same company, so that share identification rules (see Tolley's Capital Gains Tax under Shares and Securities—Identification Rules) are applied separately to ISA investments (and separately as between different

ISAs held by the same investor). The normal share reorganisation rules are disapplied in respect of ISA investments in the event of a reorganisation of share capital involving an allotment for payment, e.g. a rights issue. Shares transferred to an ISA in the limited circumstances described above are deemed for these purposes to have been ISA investments from, in the case of SAYE option scheme shares, their acquisition by the investor, in the case of all-employee plan shares, their ceasing to be subject to the plan, and, in the case of profit sharing scheme shares, the earlier of the release date (see 82.19 SHARE-RELATED EMPLOYMENT INCOME AND EXEMPTIONS) and the date on which the investor instructed the scheme trustees to transfer ownership of the shares to him. Where the investor held shares eligible for transfer to an ISA and other shares of the same class but not so eligible, disposals are generally identified primarily with the latter, thus preserving to the greatest possible extent the eligibility of the remaining shares.

Qualifying investments for the various ISA components are as follows.

Stocks and shares component. Qualifying investments for a stocks and shares component are as follows.

(*a*) Shares issued by a company (other than an investment trust, but see (*e*) below) wherever incorporated, and officially listed on a recognised stock exchange (see below). There are rules to allow the official listing condition to be treated as satisfied in the case of shares issued under a public offer and due to be listed.

(*b*) Securities (i.e. secured or unsecured loan stock and similar) issued by a company wherever incorporated, and with a minimum residual term of five years from the date when first held under the ISA. Either the securities must be officially listed on a recognised stock exchange (see below) or the shares in the issuing company or its 75% holding company must be so listed. In the case of securities of an investment trust, the trust must satisfy the two qualifying conditions at (*e*) below.

(*c*) Gilt-edged securities and gilt strips with at least five years to run to maturity from the date when first held under the ISA.

(*d*) Securities issued by or on behalf of a government of a European Economic Area State (comprising the EU plus Norway, Iceland and Liechtenstein and excluding for this purpose the UK), and strips of such securities, with at least five years to run to maturity from the date when first held under the ISA.

(*e*) Shares in a qualifying investment trust listed in the Official List of the Stock Exchange. Broadly, in order to qualify, an investment trust must have no 'eligible rental income' (within *ICTA 1988, s 508A* — see Tolley's Corporation Tax under Unit and Investment Trusts) *and* not more than 50% in value of its investments can be securities otherwise within any of (*b*)–(*d*) above but having less than five years to run to maturity from the date when first acquired by the trust.

(*f*) (Before 6 April 2004) units in, or shares of,

- a securities scheme (broadly an authorised unit trust or open-ended investment company ('OEIC') or part of an umbrella scheme — see 90.1 UNIT TRUSTS), or
- a warrant scheme (broadly a type of authorised unit trust or OEIC investing in warrants or part of an umbrella scheme of that category), or
- a relevant UCITS (an Undertaking for Collective Investment in Transferable Securities situated in and authorised by an EU Member State other than the UK, or part of such an undertaking equivalent to part of an umbrella scheme),

where the scheme or UCITS satisfies the equivalent of the 50% condition in (*e*) above.

(*fa*) (After 5 April 2004) units in, or shares of,

- a securities scheme (as in (*f*) above), or
- a warrant scheme (as in (*f*) above), or
- a relevant UCITS (an Undertaking for Collective Investment in Transferable Securities situated in and authorised by an EU Member State other than the UK, or part of such an undertaking equivalent to part of an umbrella scheme), or
- a fund of funds scheme (as defined),

where the units or shares satisfy the '5% test' outlined below.

(*g*) (Before 6 April 2004) units in, or shares of, a fund of funds scheme (as defined), subject to the condition that not more than 50% in value of its investments can be investments which would otherwise be within (*f*) above but do not themselves satisfy the 50% condition therein mentioned.

(*ga*) (After 16 November 2003) units in, or shares of, a Chapter 5 UCITS (an Undertaking for Collective Investment in Transferable Securities complying with Chapter 5 of the Collective Investment Schemes Sourcebook made by the Financial Services Authority) where the units or shares satisfy the '5% test' outlined below.

(*h*) Shares acquired by the investor under a SAYE share option scheme or all-employee share ownership plan or appropriated to him under an approved profit sharing scheme which are transferred into the ISA as mentioned under '*General*' above.

(*j*) (From 13 December 2000) a 'depositary interest' in or in relation to an investment which is itself a qualifying investment other than cash. A '*depositary interest*' means the rights of any person to investments held by another, effectively as his nominee. After 16 November 2003 or 5 April 2004 (as appropriate), the underlying investment, if within (*fa*) or (*ga*) above, must satisfy the '5% test' outlined below.

(*k*) (From 6 April 2005) units in a relevant collective investment scheme specified as a stakeholder product by *SI 2004 No 2738, reg 5* (the *Financial Services and Markets Act 2000 (Stakeholder Products) Regulations 2004*) where the units satisfy the '5% test' outlined below.

(*l*) Life insurance policies issued on or after 6 April 2005 which satisfy the conditions summarised below under Insurance component and which also satisfy the '5% test' outlined below.

(*m*) (From 6 April 2005) life insurance policies previously held in an insurance component and transferred to the stocks and shares component under the transitional provisions following abolition of the insurance component (see below under Insurance component).

(*n*) Cash held on deposit pending investment in any of the above.

By concession, before 22 July 2004, a fund of funds scheme that invested in a Chapter 5 UCITS was eligible for inclusion in an ISA if the Chapter 5 UCITS restricted its investment and borrowing powers to those of a securities scheme (Revenue PEP and ISA Bulletin No 13, 10 December 2003). On and after 22 July 2004, such investment is permitted in any case and the concession is withdrawn (Revenue PEP and ISA Bulletin No 16, 2 July 2004).

The term '*company*' does not for the above purposes include an OEIC, a UCITS or an industrial and provident society (or 51% subsidiary thereof).

As regards the 50% test in (*e*) (and consequently (*f*) and (*g*)) above, securities transferred under stock lending arrangements are still considered to be held by the trust or scheme, and any collateral obtained under those arrangements is ignored (Revenue PEP and ISA Bulletin No 5, 29 April 2002).

For the purposes of (*fa*), (*ga*), (*j*), (*k*) and (*l*) above, an investment satisfies the '*5% test*' if there is no time during the five years after the investment becomes held in the ISA when, by virtue of any contract or any other transaction entered into or by virtue of the nature of the underlying investments, the investor is not exposed (or not exposed to any significant extent) to the risk of a loss (from fluctuations in value) exceeding 5% of the sum of the capital consideration paid (or payable) for the acquisition of the investment and the incidental costs of acquisition. Thus, if the investor is certain or near certain of receiving back at least 95% of the investment within five years, for example if he is given a guarantee to that effect or if the product itself invests substantially in cash, the test is failed. Where a life insurance policy confers an option to have its terms changed or have a new policy issued in its place, any such potential change is taken into account in applying the 5% test.

Investments held in an ISA on 6 April 2004 and within (*f*) or (*g*) above may continue to be held in the ISA notwithstanding the '5% test' introduced in (*fa*) above. The same applies to depositary interests (see (*j*) above) where the underlying investment is within (*f*) or (*g*) above.

Following a revision in the Revenue's interpretation of the phrase 'listed on a recognised stock exchange', securities admitted to trading on a European Economic Area exchange where securities traded are not listed by the relevant competent authority may have ceased to be a qualifying investment from 28 November 2001. Amending regulations were passed to preserve the qualifying status of securities held on that date within an ISA (where such status would otherwise have been lost for the aforementioned reason and no other) for as long as the above circumstances continue (and see Revenue Press Release 28 November 2001).

Cash component. Qualifying investments for a cash component are as follows.

(i) Cash deposited in a deposit account with a building society, a person within *ICTA 1988, s 840A(1)(b)* (see 7.1 BANKS) or certain European institutions entitled to accept deposits in the UK.

(ii) Cash deposited in a building society share account.

(iii) Units in, or shares of, a money market scheme (as defined).

(iv) Units in, or shares of, a fund of funds scheme (as defined) which permits investment only in units in, or shares of, money market schemes.

(v) Designated national savings products.

(vi) (After 16 November 2003) investments that would fall within (*ga*) above (stocks and shares component) but for their failing the '5% test'.

(vii) (After 16 November 2003) depositary interests (see (*j*) above) in or in relation to an investment which is itself a qualifying investment for a cash component.

(viii) (After 5 April 2004) investments that would fall within (*fa*) above (stocks and shares component) but for their failing the '5% test'.

(ix) (After 5 April 2005) a deposit account specified as a stakeholder product by *SI 2004 No 2738, reg 4* (the *Financial Services and Markets Act 2000 (Stakeholder Products) Regulations 2004*).

(x) (After 5 April 2005) units in a relevant collective investment scheme specified as a stakeholder product by *SI 2004 No 2738, reg 5* that would fall within (*k*) above (stocks and shares component) but for their failing the '5% test'.

(xi) Life insurance policies issued after 5 April 2005 that would fall within (*l*) above (stocks and shares component) but for their failing the '5% test'.

(xii) (After 5 April 2005) life insurance policies previously held in an insurance component and transferred to the cash component under the transitional provisions following abolition of the insurance component (see below under Insurance component).

A deposit or share account within (i) or (ii) above is not a qualifying investment if is 'connected' with any other account held within those categories (whether or not by the investor). For this purpose, accounts are '*connected*' if either was opened with reference to the other or with a view to enabling the other to be opened, or facilitating the opening of the other, on particular terms *and* the terms on which the cash component account was opened would have been significantly less favourable to the investor if the other had not been opened. The Revenue will accept that an account is not a connected account if it is a 'feeder' account opened to enable investors to fund future deposits into an ISA, provided that the interest on the feeder account is in line with the interest paid on the account manager's other savings accounts (see Revenue Guidance Notes for ISA Managers).

Insurance component. Qualifying investments for an insurance component are policies of life insurance satisfying specified conditions and cash held on deposit pending investment in such policies. The insurance must be on the life of the ISA investor only and its terms and conditions must provide:

(A) that the policy may only be owned or held as a qualifying investment for an ISA insurance component;

(B) that, if found to be in breach of (A) above, it shall automatically terminate (and see also above under 'Tax exemptions');

(C) for an express prohibition of any transfer to the investor of the policy or the rights conferred thereby or any share or interest therein (other than cash proceeds on termination or partial surrender); and

(D) that the policy etc. cannot be assigned other than by transfer of title between approved ISA managers or by its vesting in the investor's personal representatives.

The policy must constitute life insurance and must not be a contract to pay a life annuity, a personal portfolio bond (see 45.13 LIFE ASSURANCE POLICIES) or a contract constituting pension business (as defined). There must be no contractual obligation to pay any premium other than the first (so regular premium policies are excluded). 'Connected' policies are excluded in much the same way as connected accounts are excluded from a cash component (see above). The making of loans by, or by arrangement with, the insurer to, or at the direction of, the ISA investor is prohibited.

For 2005/06 onwards, the insurance component is abolished, but the same conditions as above apply to determine whether or not a policy is a qualifying investment for a stocks and shares component (see (*l*) above) or a cash component (see (xi) above). For these purposes, a '*policy*' includes rights under a linked long-term contract specified as a stakeholder product by *SI 2004 No 2738, reg 6* (the *Financial Services and Markets Act 2000 (Stakeholder Products) Regulations 2004*).

Under transitional provisions, policies held in an insurance component immediately before 6 April 2005 are transferred to one of the remaining components as follows. If all the policies were issued before 6 April 2004, they are transferred to the stocks and shares component in the case of a maxi-account or redesignated as a stocks and shares component in the case of a mini-account (the maximum subscription to a stocks and shares component having been increased by £1,000 from 6 April 2005, principally to accommodate this). If any of the policies were issued after 5 April 2004, the 5% test (see above under Stocks and shares component) is applied to those policies, but on a once and for all basis on 6 April 2005 (i.e. disregarding the reference in the 5% test to the five years after the investment becomes held in the ISA); if they all pass that test, the foregoing applies, but if any of them fail, they are all transferred to the cash component or redesignated as a cash component. Where the investor wishes to continue paying into a pre-6 April 2005 policy, the changes may affect his ability to do so, due to the general rules above denying subscriptions to more than one ISA of the same component in any one tax year (see Revenue PEP and ISA Bulletin No 17, 17 November 2004).

Repairing of invalid accounts. Where, within a single tax year, an investor opens a valid ISA, closes it and opens a new ISA of the same designation and component, the new ISA used to be technically invalid (because transfers between ISAs can only be carried out by account managers). For 2003/04 onwards, where the account is a mini-account or TESSA only account, the new ISA (i.e. the first such ISA to be opened after the said closure and in the same tax year) is treated as valid (and thus qualifying for tax relief) from the date it is opened.

Where the above circumstances occurred in 2001/02 or 2002/03 and the Revenue give notice after 7 January 2003 that the new account is invalid, the account becomes 'eligible for repair', i.e. it qualifies for tax relief *but only from the date of the notice*. Similar consequences ensue for 2001/02 and all subsequent years (where the resulting Revenue notice is given after 7 January 2003) where an investor subscribes to an incompatible combination of maxi-accounts and mini-accounts in a single tax year. Accounts thus eligible for repair are the earliest invalid account opened in the year and any account to which the capital proceeds of a matured TESSA are transferred. Repairing of accounts is subject to normal subscription limits, and where necessary the Revenue will apportion (i.e. between valid accounts and any one or more accounts eligible for repair) the total amount subscribed in the tax year.

Account managers. The regulations cover qualification as an account manager, Revenue approval and withdrawal thereof, appointment of UK tax representatives of non-UK account managers, account managers ceasing to act or to qualify, claims for tax relief and agreement of liabilities, annual returns of income and of information, annual and interim tax repayment claims, record-keeping, and information to be provided to investors.

[*SI 1998 No 1870; SI 1998 No 3174; SI 2000 Nos 809, 3112; SI 2001 No 908; SI 2001 No 3629, Articles 168–178; SI 2001 No 3778; SI 2002 Nos 453, 1974, 3158; SI 2003 No 2747; SI 2004 Nos 1677, 2996; SI 2005 No 609*].

Separate regulations modify existing tax legislation so far as it concerns individual savings account business of insurance companies. [*SI 1998 No 1871 as amended; SI 1998 No 3174; SI 2001 No 3629, Article 179*].

Closure and death. Subject to the ISA terms and conditions, an investor may close an ISA at any time without affecting tax exemptions up to the date of closure. Where an investor dies, income and gains in respect of ISA investments which arise after the date of death but before the date of closure are not exempt.

See generally Revenue Booklet IR 2008 and the Revenue 'Guidance Notes for ISA Managers'. There is also a Revenue ISA helpline on 0845-604 1701, and PEP and ISA Bulletins are published on the Revenue website.'

28.24 **Personal Equity Plans.** *SI 2004 No 1676* is added to the list of statutory references at the end.

35 Inland Revenue: Administration

35.1 **Introduction.** The final paragraph is updated to read as follows.

'**HM Revenue and Customs (HMRC).** The Chancellor of the Exchequer announced in his Budget speech on 17 March 2004 that the Inland Revenue and HM Customs & Excise are to merge. The new department will be known as HM Revenue and Customs (HMRC) and is expected to be in operation from Spring 2005. A draft advice note ('HMRC powers and your rights') was published for consultation in December 2004 and sets out how the creation of the integrated department will affect taxpayers in their day-to-day dealings with HMRC officers. The integrated department will include a new Small Business Unit (Revenue Press Release 2 December 2004).'

35.14 **Revenue functions carried out by the Assets Recovery Agency.** The following paragraph is added at the end.

'See the Assets Recovery Agency's website at www.assetsrecovery.gov.uk and the guidance at www.inlandrevenue.gov.uk/specialist/ara-guidance_.pdf'

37 Inland Revenue Explanatory Publications

37.1 **Inland Revenue explanatory pamphlets.** The following new and updated pamphlets are included in the list:

IR 10 Paying the Right Tax on Your Earnings or Pension (August 2004).
IR 45 Contacting the Inland Revenue when Someone has Died (February 2005).
IR 87 Letting and Your Home (including 'Rent a Room') (September 2004).
IR 111 Bank and Building Society Interest — Are You Paying Tax When You Don't Need To? (August 2004).
IR 115 Childcare provided by employers (February 2005).
IR 141 Open Government (July 2004).
IR 152 Trusts — An Introduction (September 2004).
IR 160 Inland Revenue Enquiries under Self-Assessment (August 2004).
IR 2008 ISAs and PEPs (January 2005).
COP 11 Self-Assessment: Local Office Enquiries (October 2004).
E24 (2005) Tips, Gratuities, Service Charges and Troncs (February 2005).
WTC5 Child Tax Credit and Working Tax Credit — Help with the Costs of Childcare (June 2004).
WTC6 Child Tax Credit and Working Tax Credit — Other Types of Help You May Be Able To Get (August 2004).

The following are deleted from the list.

IR 33 Income Tax and School Leavers (May 2000).
IR 60 Income Tax and Students (June 2002).

In the paragraph at the end of the chapter, concerning the Revenue Tax Bulletin, the penultimate sentence is updated to read as follows.

'Telephone enquiries can be made on 020–7147 2335 (subscription or distribution) and 020–7147 2317 (more general information).'

38 Inland Revenue Extra-Statutory Concessions

The following new concession is added.

A104 **Car and fuel benefits** provided to employees via vouchers or credit tokens are no longer double counted, as from 5 July 2004, in determining whether or not the employment is 'lower paid' (Revenue Press Release 5 July 2004). See 75.14 SCHEDULE E—EMPLOYMENT INCOME.

39 Inland Revenue Press Releases

The following press release is added.

4.3.05 **Transfer pricing.** With effect from today, *Finance Act 2005* will extend the transfer pricing rules to further prevent businesses obtaining a tax advantage from non-arm's length transactions with persons who control the business; the rules apply to the financing arrangements of a business in two additional circumstances. See 3.8 ANTI-AVOIDANCE.

40 Inland Revenue Statements of Practice

The following new Statement of Practice is added.

SP 3/04 **Double tax relief — Yugoslavia.** Details are given as to the application of the UK/Yugoslavia double tax agreement to the countries formerly known as Yugoslavia. See 24.2 DOUBLE TAX RELIEF.

41 Interest on Overpaid Tax

41.1 **1996/97 onwards (self-assessment).** The following entries are added to the list of rates.

2.5% p.a. from 6 December 2003 to 5 September 2004

3.5% p.a. from 6 September 2004

41.2 **1995/96 and earlier years.** Identical additions are made as in 41.1 above.

42 Interest and Surcharges on Unpaid Tax

42.1 **Interest on unpaid tax.** The following entries are added to the list of rates.

6.5% p.a. from 6 December 2003 to 5 September 2004

7.5% p.a. from 6 September 2004

44 Interest Receivable

44.3A The following new paragraph is added.

'Any interest element included in a compensation package for the *mis-selling of certain financial products*, such as mortgage endowment policies, is normally taxable under SCHEDULE D, CASE III (72) under general principles. If the package includes a payment for personal injury, interest on such payment is tax-exempt by virtue of 28.16(i) EXEMPT INCOME. Interest on compensation for mis-sold pensions is specifically exempted (see 28.5 EXEMPT INCOME). (Revenue Tax Bulletin August 2004 pp 1131, 1132).'

46 Losses

46.8 **Restrictions on relief.** At the end of sub-paragraph (*f*) (losses derived from film tax reliefs), the following paragraph is added.

'*FA 2005* will include provisions, backdated to (broadly) 2 December 2004, excluding from an individual's capital contribution, for the above purposes, any amount to the extent that any arrangement exists whereby the cost of providing that amount is, or could be, borne by another person (Pre-Budget Report, 2 December 2004).'

51 Non-Residents and Other Overseas Matters

51.1 **Limit on income chargeable on non-residents.** At the end, the following paragraph is added.

'The Revenue announced on 21 December 2004 that they may have made errors in cases where a non-resident higher rate taxpayer is in receipt of an annuity under a retirement annuity contract and has left the tax calculation to the Revenue; the annuity may not have been identified as 'excluded income' as required by (*d*) above. They ask practitioners to contact the tax office of any client they think may have overpaid tax as a result of such error; tax repayments will be made for 1996/97 onwards. For 2004/05 and subsequent years' returns, the Revenue should be asked for a manual calculation in such cases.'

51.7 **Non-resident entertainers and sportsmen.** The second paragraph is amended to read as follows.

'A '*relevant activity*' is an activity performed in the UK by an entertainer or sportsman in his character as such on or in connection with (including promotion of) a commercial occasion or event (including participation in live or recorded transmissions of any kind) for which he is entitled to receive a payment or transfer or which is designed to promote commercial sales or activity by any means. See *Set, Deuce and Ball v Robinson (Sp C 373), [2003] SSCD 382* which analysed this definition in relation to non-resident tennis players performing at Wimbledon; on appeal, the CA held that payments are *not* within the scope of these provisions if made by a foreign company with no UK tax presence (*Agassi v Robinson CA 2004, [2005] STC 303*).'

51.10 **Personal allowances for certain non-residents.** The final paragraph is replaced with the following two paragraphs.

'Claims should be made on Form R43 to Inland Revenue, Centre for Non-Residents, Fitz Roy House, PO Box 46, Nottingham, England, NG2 1BD. A right of appeal to the Special Commissioners, within three months of the notice of the Board's decision, is given by *TMA 1970, Sch 1A paras 9(2), 10*.

See www.inlandrevenue.gov.uk/cnr/r43-notes-2005.pdf (in particular note 3) for more detail, including a list of those countries whose nationals and/or residents may be entitled to allowances under double tax treaties.'

52 Offshore Funds

52.1 **Introduction.** At the end of the second paragraph, the following is added.

'For a review of the offshore funds legislation with particular reference to changes made by *FA 2004* (as referred to in this chapter where appropriate), see Revenue Tax Bulletin October 2004 pp 1152–1155.'

52.2 **Offshore funds operating equalisation arrangements.** After the second paragraph (containing a definition of 'equalisation arrangements'), the following paragraph is added.

'Where a sub-fund or class of interest is treated as a fund in its own right (see 52.3 below), this definition applies with appropriate modifications (see *SI 2004 No 2572, reg 3*).'

52.3 **Material interests in offshore funds.** The last paragraph on page 588 is replaced with the following.

'For account periods (see 52.4 below) ending on or after 22 July 2004, sub-funds of a main fund (the umbrella fund) and different classes of interest in a main fund constitute separate offshore funds. This allows the test for distributing status (see 52.5 below) to be applied to them independently. The offshore funds legislation is appropriately modified in its application to such sub-funds and classes of interest (see *SI 2004 No 2572*).'

52.4 **Non-qualifying offshore funds.** At the end of sub-paragraph (C) on page 591, a reference is added to *SI 2004 No 2572, reg 4(1)(6)*.

52.5 **The distribution test.** At the end of both the fourth paragraph (beginning 'A fund is treated as pursuing …' and the following paragraph, a reference is added to *SI 2004 No 2572, reg 4(1)(2)*.

At the end of the paragraph on page 593 beginning 'The special corporation tax rules …'. the following is added.

'Where, in a case where no election has been made, a new sub-fund or class of interest is established *after* 22 July 2004 and is regarded as a separate offshore fund by virtue of 52.3 above, the change in treatment does not apply to the sub-fund or class either, so that they always take the same treatment as the 'parent' fund.'

At the end, a reference is added to *SI 2004 No 2572, regs 4(1)(5), 6 & 7*.

52.6 **Modifications of distribution test.** At the end of sub-paragraphs (*a*), (*c*) and (*d*), references are added to, respectively, *SI 2004 No 2572, reg 4(1)(3)*, *SI 2004 No 2572, reg 4(1)(4)* and *SI 2004 No 2572, reg 4(1)(6)*.

52.7 **Certification procedure.** At the end of the paragraph spanning pages 595, 596, a reference is added to *SI 2004 No 2572, reg 4(1)(7)*.

52.11 **Disposals involving an equalisation element.** At the end of both the first and second paragraphs, a reference is added to *SI 2004 No 2572, reg 5*.

53 Partnerships

53.9 **Non-active partners: restriction of loss reliefs and interest relief.** Immediately before the first full paragraph on page 612, the following paragraph is added.

'*FA 2005* will include provisions, backdated to (broadly) 2 December 2004, excluding from a partner's capital contribution, for the above purposes, any amount to the extent that any arrangement exists whereby the cost of providing that amount is, or could be, borne by another person (Pre-Budget Report, 2 December 2004).'

53.17 **Limited partnerships.** At the end, the following paragraph is added.

'*FA 2005* will include provisions, backdated to (broadly) 2 December 2004, excluding from a partner's capital contribution, for the above purposes, any amount to the extent that any arrangement exists whereby the cost of providing that amount is, or could be, borne by another person (Pre-Budget Report, 2 December 2004).'

53.18 **Limited liability partnerships (LLPs).** Immediately above the paragraph on page 620 headed 'Investment LLPs and property investment LLPs', the following paragraph is added.

'*FA 2005* will include provisions, backdated to (broadly) 2 December 2004, excluding from a partner's capital contribution, for the above purposes, any amount to the extent that any arrangement exists whereby the cost of providing that amount is, or could be, borne by another person (Pre-Budget Report, 2 December 2004).'

55 Pay As You Earn

55.9 **PAYE returns.** The section on mandatory e-filing (spanning pages 634, 635) is updated to read as follows.

'**Mandatory e-filing.** The Commissioners of Inland Revenue have been given extremely wide powers to make regulations requiring the use of electronic communications for the delivery of information required or authorised to be delivered under tax legislation. [*FA 2002, ss 135, 136*]. The Government has adopted a three-stage move towards e-filing of PAYE returns (i.e. the information required at (*a*) above), as follows.

(A) Employers with 250 or more employees are required to file electronically from 2004/05.

(B) Employers with 50 or more employees are required to file electronically from 2005/06.

(C) Employers with less than 50 employees are required to file electronically from 2009/10, with an incentive for earlier adoption.

(Revenue/C&E Budget Press Release 2/02, 17 April 2002).

Under the regulations giving effect to (A) and (B) above, the mandatory e-filing requirement applies for 2004/05 to employers who at 26 October 2003 were 'large employers' (i.e. they were paying PAYE income to at least 250 recipients) and who received an e-filing notice issued by the Revenue no later than 31 December 2003. Similar provisions apply for subsequent years but by reference to employers who at the specified date (to be announced by Revenue Direction, e.g. 24 October 2004 for 2005/06) were 'large or medium-sized employers' (i.e. they were paying PAYE income to at least 50 recipients) and who received an e-filing notice issued by the Revenue no later than 31 December preceding the tax year in question. An appeal may be made (within 30 days) against an e-filing notice on the grounds that the employer does not fall into the specified category. There are let-outs for members of any religious orders whose beliefs are incompatible with electronic communication. Penalties for failure to comply range from £600 to £3,000 depending upon the number of employees required to be included in the returns, the maximum penalty applying where there are 1,000 or more. Appeals may be made against penalty determinations on specified grounds including reasonable excuse throughout the default period. [*SI 2003 No 2682, regs 190, 191, 205–210; Revenue Directions 21 October 2003, 29 September 2004*]. For 2004/05 only, the penalty will be based on the number of employees at 26 October 2003, though on appeal the employer can insist on it being calculated on the statutory basis instead (Revenue Tax Bulletin August 2004 p 1137).

Although in-year PAYE returns can be filed online from April 2005 onwards, the Revenue do not insist on electronic filing where the returns cover the part of the tax year ending with the date of an insolvency event (e.g. liquidation, receivership, administration or bankruptcy); no online filing penalty will be charged in these circumstances provided a late filing penalty (see 57.9 PENALTIES) does not fall to be charged (Revenue Tax Bulletin October 2004 p 1158).

Regulations have also been made to give effect to (C) above. The incentives are available to employers who at a specified date (to be announced by Revenue Direction) preceding the tax year in question were 'small employers' (i.e. they were paying PAYE income to less than 50 recipients) or who first started paying PAYE income after that date. The payments receivable are £250 for each of 2004/05 and 2005/06, £150 for 2006/07, £100 for 2007/08 and £75 for 2008/09. These are not chargeable to tax. Appeals are possible (within 30 days of the notice) against an officer's decision not to make an incentive payment or to recover a payment already made. [*SI 2003 No 2495; Revenue Direction 21 October 2003*]. Employers can either use incentive payments to reduce a subsequent PAYE liability or claim a repayment, but repayments will not be sent to the employer's agent (Revenue Tax Bulletin February 2004 p 1085).

All returns filed online must meet the Quality Standard and will otherwise be rejected and treated as not having been filed; see www.inlandrevenue.gov.uk/ebu/qual_stand.htm and Revenue Tax Bulletin August 2004 p 1137.

See also Revenue Tax Bulletins February 2003 pp 995, 996, February 2004 pp 1084, 1085 and Revenue Handbook 'Do it online: online filing and electronic payment handbook' available at www.inlandrevenue.gov.uk/employers/doitonline.pdf'

55.42 **Tips, organised arrangements for sharing.** The final paragraph is updated to read as follows.

'See generally Revenue Employment Procedures Manual EP 1155 *et seq.*, Revenue booklet E24 (2005) 'Tips, Gratuities, Service Charges and Troncs' (available at www.inlandrevenue.gov.uk/helpsheets/e24.pdf) and Revenue Tax Bulletin February 2004 pp 1081–1084.'

56 Payment of Tax

56.11 **Recovery of tax paid under mistake of law.** At the end, the following paragraph is added.

'As it transpired, the Ch D in *Deutsche Morgan Grenfell* was reversed by the CA, which held that the mistake of law rules had no application in a case involving an unlawful demand for tax. In any such case, restitution can be achieved only under the principle established in *Woolwich* above. In the instant case, the six-year period limitation was held to run from the time of the original payment of tax to the time the claim for restitution was made. (*Deutsche Morgan Grenfell Group plc v CIR CA, 2005 STI 194*).'

57 Penalties

57.4 **Failure to produce documents.** At the end, the following is added: 'For a successful appeal against penalty notices containing basic errors, see *Austin v Price (Sp C 426), [2004] SSCD 487*.'

57.19 **Liability under criminal law.** A reference is added to the Revenue's website at www.inlandrevenue.gov.uk/prosecutions/prosecution-policy.htm as regards their policy towards criminal prosecution for offences.

58 Pension Income

58.2 **Taxable income.** At the end of sub-paragraph (*c*), the following is added.

'After 5 April 2005, it will be possible to defer the State pension and take a taxable lump sum. Tax will be applied to the lump sum at the individual's marginal tax rate, and it will not affect any age-related allowances due. Claimants will be able to self-declare their marginal rate, and tax will be deducted at source. (Pre-Budget Report, 2 December 2004, para 5.71).'

58.3 **General exemptions.** At the end of sub-paragraph (*a*), the following is added.

'See 58.2(*c*) above re lump sums taken in connection with the *State* pension, which *are* taxable.'

59 Pension Provision after 5 April 2006

59.2 **Registered pension schemes.** At the end, the following is added.

'The Financial Secretary to the Treasury announced in October 2004 that from the outset, registered pension schemes will be required to send forms online and make payments electronically.'

60 Personal Pension Schemes (and Stakeholder Pensions)

60.3 **Limits of relief.** It is noted that the earnings cap for 2005/06 will be £105,600 as announced in the Pre-Budget Report on 2 December 2004.

61 Personal Service Companies etc.

61.5 **Intermediaries to which these provisions apply.** A reference is made to Revenue Tax Bulletin December 2004 pp 1165–1168 for more on composite service companies and also on managed service companies (i.e. one-worker service companies set up and run by a promoter for an administration fee).

61.8 **Computation of deemed employment payment.** A reference is made to Revenue Tax Bulletin December 2004 pp 1166–1168 for notes on the deductibility of travel and subsistence expenses reimbursed to workers in a composite service company or managed service company.

65 Residence, Ordinary Residence and Domicile

65.1 **Introduction.** The final paragraph is updated to read as follows.

'**Possible future changes?** In the 2002 Budget, the Government announced a review of the residence and domicile rules as they affect the taxation of individuals. A year later, in April 2003, a background paper was published on the subject, but this does little more than describe the current rules and outline the underlying principles to which any changes should adhere; it contains no specific proposals. According to the 2004 Pre-Budget Report (para 5.101), the Government 'is considering various aspects of this issue', 'remains determined to proceed' and 'would welcome further contributions to the debate, which will then be taken forward by the publication of a consultation paper setting out possible approaches to reform'.'

66 Retirement Annuities

66.5 **Unused relief carried forward.** At the end, a reference is inserted to *Lonsdale v Braisby Ch D, [2004] STC 1606*.

67 Retirement Schemes for Employees

67.4 **Conditions for approval after 5 April 1973.** At the end of sub-paragraph (*f*), it is noted that the figure of £100,000 is to be increased to £105,600 for 2005/06 (per Pre-Budget Report, 2 December 2004). It is also noted at the foot of page 747 that the permitted maximum is to be similarly increased.

68 Returns

68.2 **Annual returns of income and chargeable gains.** The following paragraph is added.

'Under new criteria applicable to returns for 2004/05 and subsequent years, fewer taxpayers (including higher rate taxpayers) whose affairs can be adequately dealt with using the PAYE system will be asked to complete a return, though they may choose to do so if they wish. See Guidelines for Individuals completing Tax Returns at www.inlandrevenue.gov.uk/sa/guidelines.htm and at www.inlandrevenue.gov.uk/sa/guidelines-sa-returns.htm and 'frequently asked questions' at www.inlandrevenue.gov.uk/sa/faqs-sa-returns.htm'

68.14 **Electronic lodgement of tax returns etc.** It is noted that the electronic lodgement service is to continue until at least April 2006 (for 2004/05 returns) (Revenue 'Working Together' Bulletin August 2004 p 2).

68.15 **Bankers etc. and paying agents — returns of interest.** In the section headed 'EU Savings Directive', it is noted that the Directive is now due to come into force on 1 July 2005.

Again in the section headed 'EU Savings Directive', the sentence beginning 'See the Revenue's detailed Savings Income Reporting Guidance Notes' is replaced with the following:

'For detailed savings income reporting guidance prepared by the Revenue plus notes for UK investors and other related items, see www.inlandrevenue.gov.uk/esd-guidance/index.htm'

69 Schedule A—Property Income

69.5 **Deductions — miscellaneous.** In sub-paragraph (*e*) (Landlord's expenditure on energy-saving items), it is noted that the *regulations* are now available — see *SI 2004 No 2664*. It is made clear that the £1,500 maximum applies per building, irrespective of the number of persons eligible to claim a deduction in respect of that building.

71 Schedule D, Cases I and II—Profits of Trades etc.

71.30 **General.** In the section on 'Adjustments on change of basis', the following paragraph is added after the first paragraph.

'For periods of account beginning after 31 December 2004, under proposed legislation in *FA 2005*, a '*change of basis*' will also include a change from using UK GAAP (see above under True and fair view requirement) to using international accounting standards (Pre-Budget Report, 2 December 2004).'

71.34 **Bad and doubtful debts.** At the end of the para beginning 'The provision for a bad or doubtful debt', the following is added:

'It is not possible to employ hindsight to revisit a past computation of taxable profit so as to provide for a debt in a period of account in which there was no evidence that it would eventually prove to be bad (*Thompson v CIR (Sp C 458), 2005 STI 222*).'

71.44 **Employees (and directors).** After the paragraph on page 843 beginning 'Payments in addition to the statutory payment', the following paragraph is added.

'A gratuitous payment made on partial cessation of a company's trade to a managing director who nevertheless continued thereafter to be a director was held non-deductible in *Relkobrook Ltd v Mapstone (Sp C 452), 2005 STI 158*.'

71.47 **Farming and market gardening.** At the end, the following is added as new sub-paragraph (*n*).

'**Woodlands grants.** The Forestry Commission's Woodland Grant Scheme (WGS) provides grants for the establishment and maintenance of WOODLANDS (94). These grants are not taxable. Where the woodland concerned is being established on agricultural land, WGS participants can also apply to join the Farm Woodland Premium Scheme (FWPS). This is administered by the Department for Environment, Food and Rural Affairs (Defra)and provides annual payments of up to £300 per hectare for up to 15 years to the farmer to compensate for lost farming income as a result of converting the land to woodland. Because the annual payments are made in lieu of farming income, they must be included in trading profits and are chargeable to income tax. It matters not that the woodlands are likely to be commercial woodlands and thus outside the charge to income tax. (Sources: Defra and Revenue Business Income Manual BIM 55165).'

71.48 **Film and audio products.** The third paragraph on page 856 (definition of 'qualifying film') is updated to read as follows.

'For the purposes of these reliefs, a film (or tape or disc) is a '*qualifying film*' (or '*qualifying tape*' or '*qualifying disc*') if it is certified as such by the Department for Culture, Media and Sport (DCMS) under *Films Act 1985, Sch 1*, which applies certain criteria as to the British, EU or Commonwealth nature of the film etc. For more details, see the DCMS website at www.culture.gov.uk/creative_industries/film/CriteriaforBritishfilms.htm'

Immediately above the heading 'Preliminary expenditure' near the foot of page 857, the following two paragraphs are added.

'*FA 2005* will include provisions intended to thwart tax avoidance schemes which seek to achieve relief under *F(No 2)A 1992, s 42* or *F(No 2)A 1997, s 48* more than once on the same film. Provisions will also seek to ensure that relief under *F(No 2)A 1992, s 42* is limited to the total production expenditure on the film. In addition, wherever a trader claims relief under *F(No 2)A 1992, s 42* or *F(No 2)A 1997, s 48* and enters into an agreement guaranteeing him income from the exploitation of the film, the relief will be restricted to the extent, if any, that guaranteed income will arise more than 15 years after the making of the agreement. All of these provisions will have effect from, broadly, **2 December 2004**. (Pre-Budget Report, 2 December 2004).

After the current system of enhanced allowances terminates on **1 July 2005**, the Government intend to replace it with a new relief, available only to companies, for qualifying films with a total production expenditure of not more than £20 million. The current system will continue to apply, instead of the new relief, to production or acquisition expenditure incurred on films on which the first day of principal photography is before 2 July 2005, the completion date is no later than 5 April 2006 and the acquisition date (where relevant) is no later than 31 December 2006. For more details, see www.inlandrevenue.gov.uk/ctsa/tax-relief-films.pdf'

71.69 **Repairs and renewals.** At the end of sub-paragraph (*b*) (business premises), the following paragraph is added.

'From 1 October 2004, *Disability Discrimination Act 1995* requires service providers to make 'reasonable adjustments' to their premises to tackle any physical features that prevent disabled people from using their services. Whilst this does not give rise to any substantive changes to pre-existing tax treatment, the Revenue have published online some related guidance covering such matters as ramps, toilets and washing facilities, signs, hand rails, lighting, doors, lifts, steps and stairs, alterations to walls and floors, car parks and paths. See www.inlandrevenue.gov.uk/specialist/disability-act-guidance.htm'

71.70 **Research and development and Scientific research.** As stated in the text, by virtue of *FA 2004, s 53*, revenue expenditure *by a company* on research and development is not precluded from deduction by reason only of the fact that it is brought into account in determining the value of an intangible asset. It is now noted that this comes into effect for accounting periods beginning after 31 December 2004 (*SI 2004 No 3268*).

71.73 **Stock in trade and work in progress.** Immediately above the heading 'Changes in basis of valuation' on page 886, the following text is *deleted*.

'It has been suggested that an amendment by the Accounting Standards Board to FRS 5 'Reporting the Substance of Transactions' requires professional work in progress to be valued at *selling price* beginning with accounts ended on or after 23 December 2003 (Taxation Vol 152, No 3941 p 376, 22 January 2004); however, not all commentators interpret the amendment in this way (Taxation Vol 152, No 3944 p 447, 12 February 2004).'

It now appears that the accountancy bodies do *not* interpret the amendment in this way, and that their view on the matter is accepted by the Inland Revenue.

72 Schedule D, Case III—Interest Receivable

72.5 **Relevant discounted securities.** At the end of the second paragraph, the following is added.

'In a case involving a gift of securities to a spouse before 27 March 2003, said to be wholly tax motivated, the Special Commissioners rejected the Revenue's application of the *Ramsay* principle (see 3.1 ANTI-AVOIDANCE) and allowed the loss (*Campbell v CIR (Sp C 421), [2004] SSCD 396*).'

Immediately above the heading 'Accrued income scheme' on page 909, the following paragraph is added.

'**Anti-avoidance: stripped corporate bonds.** *FA 2005* will include backdated legislation 'to prevent tax avoidance by individuals and trustees liable to income tax using bonds issued by companies which have been stripped of some or all of their rights to interest. The legislation will put beyond doubt that where individuals and trustees acquire, **on or after 2 December 2004**, any rights derived from a company bond (whether rights to interest, principal repayment or a mixture of both), those rights are treated as relevant discounted securities.' (Pre-Budget Report, 2 December 2004).'

74 Schedule D, Case VI—Miscellaneous Income

74.5 **Accrued income scheme: introduction.** It is noted that the accrued income scheme is to be **reformed**; the Government is to consult on the detail, with a view to legislation being included in *FA 2006* (Pre-Budget Report, 2 December 2004).

74.18 **Accrued income scheme: variable rate bonds.** At the end of sub-paragraph (*a*)(i), a reference is added to *Cadbury Schweppes plc and another v Williams (Sp C 441), [2005] SSCD 151*.

75 Schedule E—Employment Income

75.14 **Directors and employees (other than lower-paid employees) — benefits code.** Sub-paragraph (*a*) is updated to read as follows.

'Determine the aggregate (after deducting any exempt income) of:

(i) the earnings (see 75.10 above) from the employment for that year;

(ii) the total of amounts treated as earnings for that year. This includes all amounts which would be so treated under the benefits code, disregarding the exclusion of lower-paid employees where it might otherwise apply; and

(iii) any deemed employment payment for the year under *ITEPA 2003, s 54* (see 61.7 PERSONAL SERVICE COMPANIES ETC.).

As regards (ii) above: in the case of provision of living accommodation under 75.32 below, the additional charge where cost exceeds £75,000 does not apply for this purpose, the basic charge being applied regardless of the cost. Where car or car fuel benefits are provided by means of a voucher or credit token, the legislation strictly requires both the car or fuel benefit and the voucher or token benefit to be taken into account in determining whether or not earnings are at the £8,500 level (see *Allcock v King (Sp C 396), [2004] SSCD 122*); but after 4 July 2004, in all cases where liability for the tax year in question has not yet been finalised at that date, Revenue ESC A104 ensures that the voucher or token benefit will not be so taken into account where a car or car fuel benefit would apply, thus removing the anomaly of double counting (Revenue Press Release 5 July 2004).'

75.16 **Benefits-in-kind generally.** The following is added to the list on page 948 of minor benefits exempted by *regulations*.

'(From 14 December 2004) pension information and advice given to an employee on the employer's behalf where the cash equivalent of the benefit (see below) does not in total exceed £150 for the tax year; if there is an excess over £150, the full amount is taxable and not just the excess (*SI 2004 No 3087*).'

In the paragraph on page 948 beginning '*Legal expenses*', the following is added at the end:

'Legal costs incurred by a company in proceedings to which the managing director lent his name and from which he personally benefited were held to be a taxable benefit; the fact that the company also benefited was irrelevant, except that the benefit should be restricted to that proportion of total costs which is attributed to the employee on a fair basis (*XI Software Ltd v Laing (Sp C 450), [2005] SSCD 249*).'

At the end of sub-paragraph (iv) (free or subsidised meals) spanning pages 949, 950, the following is added.

'After 13 December 2004, where the provision of subsidised meals to employees is exempt as above, the provision of those meals to others who are working at the employer's premises but are not employees of that employer is also exempt. [*SI 2002 No 205, reg 6; SI 2004 No 3087*].'

The paragraph on page 955 beginning 'Where the benefit is the *transfer of an asset*' is updated to read as follows.

'Where the benefit is the *transfer of an asset after it has been used or depreciated* since the transferor acquired it, the cost of the benefit is the market value at the time of the transfer. However, if the asset (not a car or van) was first applied for the provision of any benefit for a person or for members of his family or household by reason of his employment after 5 April 1980 and a person (whether or not the present transferee) has been chargeable to tax on its use, the cost of the benefit (unless a higher benefit is obtained by taking market value at the time of transfer) is its market value when it was first so applied less the total cash equivalents of the benefit of the *use* of the asset (see above) in the years up to and including the year of transfer. [*ITEPA 2003, s 206, Sch 7 para 32(2); ICTA 1988, s 156(3)(4)*]. For 2005/06 onwards, the second alternative does not apply to computer equipment within (xxiv) above or to cycles within (xxvi) above, with the result that the charge is always on market value at time of transfer (Revenue Internet Statement 20 February 2005).'

75.18 **Motor vehicles provided for private use.** In sub-paragraph (ii) (cars for private use: 2002/03 and subsequent years), paragraph (1) (discounts) on page 964 and the immediately preceding sentence are updated to read as follows.

'Under *SI 2001 No 1123*, reductions are accordingly provided for as follows.

(1) Cars first registered after 31 December 1997, propelled solely by diesel and meeting the European standard for cleaner cars (Council Directive 70/220/EEC, Annex 1, section 5.3.1.4, table row B): the amount of the diesel supplement (as above). For 2006/07 onwards, this discount will cease for cars registered on or after 1 January 2006 (Pre-Budget Report, 2 December 2004, para 7.42).'

In sub-paragraph (iiia) (vans for private use: 2005/06 and subsequent years), the paragraph at the top of page 968 is updated to read as follows.

'These requirements must be met throughout the tax year (or throughout that part of the tax year during which the van is available to the employee), but insignificant private use is disregarded. For some examples of what the Revenue do and do not consider to be 'insignificant' in this context, see www.inlandrevenue.gov.uk/employers/van-tax.htm or Revenue Tax Bulletin October 2004 p 1161.'

75.22 **Childcare provision.** At the end, the following two paragraphs are added.

'The £50 limit applies to the face value of the childcare voucher, i.e. disregarding associated administration costs, which are thus also brought within the exemption (Pre-Budget Report, 2 December 2004, para 5.21).

See also the Revenue's guidance at www.inlandrevenue.gov.uk/childcare'

75.24 **Sporting and recreational facilities.** At the end, the following is added.

'After 13 December 2004, where the provision of recreational facilities to employees is exempt as above, the provision of those facilities to others who are working at the employer's premises but are not employees of that employer is also exempt. [*SI 2002 No 205, reg 6; SI 2004 No 3087*].'

75.48 **Wages in lieu of notice.** The last paragraph on page 1029 is updated to read as follows.

'Payments for a period where notice is given but not in fact worked ('garden leave') are income from the employment. (See *Redundant Employee v McNally (Sp C 440), [2005] SSCD 143*)'

78 Self-Assessment

78.1 **Introduction.** The fourth paragraph on page 1035 is updated to read as follows.

'A Short Tax Return (STR) for those with relatively simple tax affairs is being piloted and is expected to be rolled out nationwide in April 2005. Also, under new criteria applicable to returns for 2004/05 and subsequent years, fewer taxpayers (including higher rate taxpayers) whose affairs can be adequately dealt with using the PAYE system will be asked to complete a tax return of any kind, though they may choose to do so if they wish. See Guidelines for Individuals completing Tax Returns at www.inlandrevenue.gov.uk/sa/guidelines.htm and www.inlandrevenue.gov.uk/sa/guidelines-sa-returns.htm and 'frequently asked questions' at www.inlandrevenue.gov.uk/sa/faqs-sa-returns.htm From April 2004, the Revenue make increased use of the telephone to resolve minor queries arising in connection with completed returns. (Revenue Tax Bulletin February 2004 pp 1079, 1080).'

81 Settlements

81.5 **Discretionary and accumulation trusts.** Sub-paragraph (iv) in the list at the top of page 1052 is updated to read as follows.

'Certain stock dividends and loans or advances written off or released which, by virtue of *ICTA 1988, s 249(6)(b)* or *s 421(1)(a)* respectively, are treated as giving rise to income of the trustees. (See also *Howell & another v Trippier CA, [2004] STC 1245* in which it was held that the Schedule F trust rate applies to stock dividends received by discretionary trusts even if treated under the terms of the settlement as a capital receipt in the hands of the trustees.)'

81.16 **Definitions etc.** In sub-paragraph (*a*) the following two paragraphs are added at the end of the coverage of the Revenue's views on settlements not involving trusts.

'The Revenue have won a case before the Special Commissioners involving the issue of a share in an information technology personal service company to a spouse and the subsequent payment of dividends, with the result that dividends paid on the wife's shareholding fell to be taxed as income of the husband (*Jones v Garnett (Sp C 432), [2005] SSCD 9*). All the necessary conditions for the existence of a 'settlement' and of 'income arising under a settlement' were held to be present; and furthermore the issue of the share to the wife was held to be a gift of a right to income (see further 81.17 below), the husband being the sole director and having sole discretion as to declaration of dividends. It should be noted that one of the two presiding Commissioners dissented from the findings of her colleague, whose casting vote as chair nevertheless prevailed.

Following *Jones v Garnett* above, the Revenue have published 'A Guide to the Settlements Legislation for Small Business Advisors' (available at www.inlandrevenue.gov.uk/practitioners/guide_sba.pdf). This 'brings together some new and existing guidance in one single publication', but, in truth, adds relatively little to what has been said before. The professional bodies have expressed disappointment at this guidance (see, for example, CIOT Press Release 24 November 2004) and have published their own guidance to members on 23 November 2004 (reproduced at 2004 STI 2446), concentrating particularly on the degree of disclosure required in tax returns to reduce the risk of a later discovery assessment (though see also 5.3 ASSESSMENTS for the Revenue's own general advice on disclosure following *Langham v Veltema*).'

82 Share-Related Employment Income and Exemptions

82.2 **General matters.** After the first paragraph on page 1069, the following paragraph is added.

'*Retrospective legislation: statement of intent.* A further package of anti-avoidance measures concerning employee shares was announced in the Pre-Budget Report on 2 December 2004; these are covered in this chapter where appropriate. Draft legislation (see www.inlandrevenue.gov.uk/pbr2004/draft-schedule.pdf) and explanatory notes (see http://www.inlandrevenue.gov.uk/pbr2004/en-clause204.pdf) were published on 3 February 2005. In addition, the Government gave notice, in a statement made by the Paymaster General, of their intention 'to deal with any arrangements that emerge in future designed to frustrate our intention that employers and employees should pay the proper amount of tax and NICs on the rewards of employment'. Where the Government become aware of such arrangements, they will move to legislate against them and, 'where necessary', such legislation will take effect from the date of this statement of intent, i.e. from 2 December 2004.'

The penultimate paragraph on page 1069 (Revenue Share Focus Newsletter) is updated to reflect the fact that the Revenue Employee Share Schemes Team is now known as the Revenue Employee Shares and Securities Unit (ESSU).

Immediately above the final paragraph of 82.2 (on page 1070), the following paragraph is added.

'*Transfer pricing.* For Revenue guidance on the implications of transfer pricing (see 3.8 ANTI-AVOIDANCE) on employee share schemes operated by UK groups of companies, see www.inlandrevenue.gov.uk/international/shareschemes.pdf'

The final paragraph is replaced with the following.

'*University and Research Institution spin-out companies.* See the 'Memorandum of Understanding between University Companies Association (UNICO) and the Inland Revenue — 14 April 2004' published on 26 April 2004. This concerns the treatment of shares acquired by university employees (usually academics) in spin-out companies in the light of the provisions described in this chapter on unapproved share schemes. Spin-outs are arrangements varying from requiring university employees to risk their own money by buying shares to rewarding those employees under the university's Intellectual Property Sharing Policy. The shares acquired by the employees in the spin-out company may be acquired wholly as an investment, wholly as a reward for services, or as a combination of both. The Memorandum describes a shareholding structure agreed with the Revenue and designed to produce certainty of tax treatment and to ensure that the employees do not incur significant tax liabilities until they realise the value of their shares.

The above is to be superseded by legislation in *FA 2005*, backdated to apply to transfers after 1 December 2004 of intellectual property by universities and publicly funded not-for-profit research institutions to spin-out companies, designed to prevent an income tax charge arising on an increase in value of the spin-out company shares due to the intellectual property transfer. See Revenue Technical Note: 'New Tax Measure to help researchers acquiring shares in spin-out companies created with universities and research institutions', published on 2 December 2004 as part of the Pre-Budget Report. Draft legislation (see www.inlandrevenue.gov.uk/drafts/clause209-draftleg.pdf) and explanatory notes (see www.inlandrevenue.gov.uk/drafts/clause209-explan-notes.pdf) were published on 10 February 2005.'

82.3 **Extended meaning of 'shares'.** The following is added after the second of the two lists.

'With effect in relation to events of charge occurring after 1 December 2004, certain rights under insurance contracts are brought within this definition of 'shares' (Pre-Budget Report, 2 December 2004).'

82.4 **Restricted shares.** Immediately below the list of three disregards at the foot of page 1072, the following paragraph is added.

'In relation to events of charge occurring after 1 December 2004, it is intended to remove the third of these disregards and to add a tax avoidance test in respect of the other two (Pre-Budget Report, 2 December 2004).'

Immediately below the paragraph headed 'Tax exemption in certain cases on acquisition' spanning pages 1073, 1074, the following paragraph is added.

'In relation to events of charge occurring after 1 December 2004, the exemption on acquisition is to be disapplied, and tax charged by reference to unrestricted market value, if the arrangements fail a tax avoidance test (Pre-Budget Report, 2 December 2004).'

The last paragraph on page 1074 is updated to read as follows.

'If the chargeable event is a disposal for less than actual market value, the chargeable amount as determined above is reduced in the proportion that the consideration given on the disposal bears to the market value of the shares. In relation to events of charge occurring after 1 December 2004, this reduction is to be disapplied if the arrangements fail a tax avoidance test or if market value has been artificially depressed within the terms of 82.8 below (Pre-Budget Report, 2 December 2004).'

In the paragraph headed 'Relief for employer national insurance contributions' on page 1075, it is noted that the date appointed was 1 September 2004 (per *SI 2004 No 1945*).

The first of the paragraphs headed 'Exception from charge' on page 1075 is updated to read as follows.

'No charge to tax arises on the occurrence of a chargeable event if the restriction in question applies to all the company's shares of the same class, all the company's shares of that class are affected by an event similar to the chargeable event (disregarding the references in (i)–(iii) above to associated persons) and *either* of the conditions below is satisfied. (The extended meaning of shares in 82.3 above does not apply for this purpose.) After 6 May 2004, there is a further requirement that the arrangements under which the right or opportunity to acquire the shares was made available did not have as one of its main purposes the avoidance of tax or national insurance contributions. In relation to events of charge occurring after 1 December 2004, this avoidance test is to be extended to any arrangements made subsequent to acquisition (Pre-Budget Report, 2 December 2004).'

82.5 **Conditional interests in shares.** At the end of paragraph headed 'Reporting requirements' spanning pages 1078, 1079, the address is updated to read: 'Inland Revenue, Employee Shares and Securities Unit, Room G52, 1 Parliament Street, London, SW1A 2BQ'. A similar update is made in paragraphs 82.7, 82.14, 82.33, 82.59 and 82.73.

82.6 **Convertible shares after FA 2003.** The paragraph headed 'Tax relief on acquisition' on page 1080 is updated to read as follows.

'In relation to acquisitions on and after 1 September 2003, for the purposes of any liability to tax in respect of the acquisition of shares (under the general charging rules at 75.39 SCHEDULE E—EMPLOYMENT INCOME, under 82.16 below (unapproved share options) or under 82.10 below (acquisition for less than market value)), the market value of the employment-related shares is to be determined as if they were not convertible shares or an interest in convertible shares. Thus, if the market value per share is £1,100 with a conversion right and would be £1,000 without the conversion right, only £1,000 is taxed; previously, any tax charge on acquisition would have been calculated by reference to the full market value (£1,100). In relation to events of charge occurring after 1 December 2004, this relief is to be disapplied, and tax charged by reference to market value as if there were an immediate and unfettered right to convert, if the arrangements fail a tax avoidance test (Pre-Budget Report, 2 December 2004).'

In the paragraph headed 'Relief for employer national insurance contributions' on page 1081, it is noted that the date appointed was 1 September 2004 (per *SI 2004 No 1945*).

82.10 **Shares acquired for less than market value.** The paragraph immediately following list (*a*) to (*d*) on page 1089 is updated to read as follows.

'If the discharge of the loan is within (*a*) or (*b*) above, the amount outstanding immediately before the discharge is taxed as employment income of the employee for the tax year of discharge, and this applies regardless of whether or not the employment has terminated. After 1 December 2004, it is proposed that where arrangements are put in place to avoid this charge, the loan will be treated as discharged when the relevant transaction occurs (Pre-Budget Report, 2 December 2004).'

82.12 **Post-acquisition benefits from shares after FA 2003.** The paragraph headed 'The charge' on page 1091 and the succeeding paragraph are updated to read as follows.

'These provisions apply if an 'associated person' (as defined at 82.4 above) receives a benefit by virtue of the ownership of 'employment-related shares', whether by him or another associated person. This is to be widened with effect after 1 December 2004 (Pre-Budget Report, 2 December 2004). The amount or market value (determined as for capital gains tax purposes) of the benefit is taxed as employment income of the employee for the tax year in which the benefit is received.

Exceptions. These provisions do not apply if the benefit is otherwise chargeable to income tax. This exception is to be subject to a tax avoidance test in relation to events occurring after 1 December 2004 (Pre-Budget Report, 2 December 2004). In addition, an exception similar to that applying on chargeable events in 82.4 above is imported into the current provisions; the provisions are disapplied if a similar benefit is received by the owners of *all* the company's shares of the same class and *either* of the conditions detailed at 82.4 above is satisfied. (The extended meaning of shares in 82.3 above does not apply for this purpose, though the term does include stock.) After 6 May 2004, there is a further requirement that the arrangements under which the right or opportunity to acquire the shares was made available did not have as one of its main purposes the avoidance of tax or national insurance contributions. In relation to events of charge occurring after 1 December 2004, this avoidance test is to be extended to any arrangements made subsequent to acquisition (Pre-Budget Report, 2 December 2004).'

82.17 **Reporting obligations.** The paragraph at the top of page 1105 is replaced with the following two paragraphs.

'Particulars should be sent to Inland Revenue, Employee Shares and Securities Unit, Room G52, 1 Parliament Street, London, SW1A 2BQ. The standard form for reporting the events listed above is Form 42; the Revenue have no obligation to issue Form 42 to employers but, in cases where they did not do so, they allowed an extension to the deadline for reporting events in 2003/04 only, i.e. such events had to be reported before 1 December 2004; see Revenue Internet Statement 4 August 2004, which also includes links to 'frequently asked questions' on the need to report events and the acceptable methods of doing so.

For 2004/05 onwards, detailed guidance is available on the reporting requirements generally and on the completion of Form 42 (see www.inlandrevenue.gov.uk/shareschemes/form42guidance.pdf). This covers *inter alia* the transferring of shares in the normal course of domestic, family or personal relationships (which is not normally a reportable event but may be so if it is employment-related). Newly-incorporated companies in which directors and other employees have acquired unrestricted shares may use a short version of the form, called Form 42 (New Companies).'

83 Social Security

83.7 **Child tax credit and working tax credit.** The 2005/06 figures, taken from the December 2004 Pre-Budget Report, are added.

83.8 **National insurance contributions.** See Budget Summary for rates/amounts of contributions due for 2005/06.

91 Venture Capital Trusts

91.2 **Conditions for approval.** The second paragraph on page 1187 is updated to read as follows.

'On a second and subsequent issue by an approved VCT, the requirements of condition (*b*) above similarly do not have to be met, in relation to the money raised by the further issue, in the accounting period of the further issue or any later accounting period ending no more than three years after the making of the further issue. In relation to shares issued after 5 April 2004, *SI 2004 No 2199, reg 14* limits the operation of this rule by stipulating that the money raised by the further issue must be for the purposes of acquiring additional investments which do fulfil condition (*b*). Where any of that money (or assets derived therefrom) is used for another purpose, then from a time immediately before that use the whole of the money raised by the issue is deemed to be included in the company's investments in applying the percentage tests in condition (*b*). If any of the money is used by the VCT to buy back its own shares, this stipulation is treated, in particular, as not fulfilled if the Board regard the purchase as not insignificant in relation to the issued ordinary share capital of the VCT or if it is made as a result of a general offer to members. If the money is raised by a successor VCT (in a merger) and used to buy shares in the merging companies, the stipulation is treated, in particular, as not fulfilled if the money so used exceeds the least of three specified limits.'

The paragraph on page 1188 headed 'Mergers' and all the text under the heading 'Winding-up' are replaced with the following text.

'**Mergers.** For mergers (as defined by *FA 2002, Sch 33 para 10*) of two or more VCTs which take place after 16 April 2002, Treasury regulations (*SI 2004 No 2199, regs 9–13*) enable the merging VCTs to retain VCT status and provide for investors in the merged VCTs who continue as investors in the successor company (as likewise defined) to retain their tax reliefs. Broadly, the shares issued to effect the merger stand in the place of the shares for which they are exchanged or in respect of which they are issued. But these rules apply only where the Board have notified their approval to the merger in advance of its taking place. The regulations lay down the detailed conditions for approval and the procedure for obtaining approval (including right of appeal against non-approval); approval will not be granted to mergers carried out other than for *bona fide* commercial reasons or as part of tax avoidance arrangements. [*FA 2002, Sch 33 Pt 2; SI 2004 No 2199*].

Winding-up. Treasury regulations (*SI 2004 No 2199, regs 3–7*) enable a VCT commencing winding-up after 16 April 2002 to retain its status as a VCT for a maximum of three years from the commencement of the winding-up. To qualify for this extension, the VCT must normally have been approved for at least three years prior to commencement of winding-up (five years in the case of VCTs first issuing shares between 6 April 2004 and 5 April 2006 inclusive). The intention is to provide a period of grace during which investors' reliefs can continue; the grace period does not, however, prevent a withdrawal of income tax investment relief (see 91.7 below) where the minimum holding period is not otherwise met (Treasury Explanatory Notes to Finance Bill 2002).

Regulations (*SI 2004 No 2199, reg 8*) also permit a VCT commencing winding-up after 16 April 2002 to transfer investments to another VCT and for such investments to be treated as meeting the requirements of a qualifying holding (see 91.3 below) in the hands of the recipient VCT to the same extent as they did in the hands of the first VCT. The transfer must be by way of arm's length bargain or for consideration not below market value, and it must occur within the period of grace referred to above and after all other reasonable endeavours to sell the investments at or near to market value have failed. No more than 7.5% of the value of investments at the commencement of winding-up can be transferred in this way.

In all cases, the winding-up must be for *bona fide* commercial reasons and not part of tax avoidance arrangements.

[*FA 2002, Sch 33 Pt 1; SI 2004 No 2199*].'

91.5 **Relief in respect of investments.** To provide greater clarity, sub-paragraph (i) is updated to read as follows.

'(for shares issued in 2004/05 and 2005/06 only) tax at the higher rate (40%) on the amount eligible for relief (regardless of whether or not the individual is a higher rate taxpayer);'

Budget Summary 16 March 2005

Note: *It must be remembered that these proposals are subject to amendment during the passage of the Finance Bill.*

PERSONAL TAXATION	2005/06	2004/05
Personal allowance		
general	£4,895	£4,745
aged 65 or over in year of assessment	£7,090	£6,830
aged 75 or over in year of assessment	£7,220	£6,950
age allowance income limit	£19,500	£18,900
minimum where income exceeds limit	£4,895	£4,745
Married couple's allowance (10% relief)		
either spouse born before 6 April 1935	£5,905	£5,725
either spouse aged 75 or over in year of assessment	£5,975	£5,795
age allowance income limit	£19,500	£18,900
minimum where income exceeds limit	£2,280	£2,210
Blind person's allowance	£1,610	£1,560
Income tax rates		
Starting rate	10%	10%
on taxable income up to	£2,090	£2,020
Basic rate	22%	22%
on taxable income from starting rate limit up to	£32,400	£31,400
Higher rate	40%	40%
on taxable income over	£32,400	£31,400
Lower rate on certain interest income	20%	20%
Lower rate on dividend income	10%	10%
Higher rate on dividend income	32.5%	32.5%

COMPANY TAXATION	FY2005	FY2004
Corporation tax rates		
All companies (except below)	30%	30%
Companies with small profits	19%	19%
— 19% rate limit	£300,000	£300,000
— marginal relief limit	£1,500,000	£1,500,000
— marginal relief fraction	11/400	11/400
— marginal rate	32.75%	32.75%
Starting rate	0%	0%
— 0% rate limit	£10,000	£10,000
— marginal relief limit	£50,000	£50,000
— marginal relief fraction	19/400	19/400
— marginal rate	23.75%	23.75%
Non-corporate distribution rate	19%	19%

CAPITAL GAINS TAX	2005/06	2004/05
Rate — general	10%*:20%*:40%*	10%*:20%*:40%*
— trustees and personal representatives	40%*	40%*
General exemption limit	£8,500	£8,200

*subject to taper relief where available

INHERITANCE TAX	Transfers after 5/4/2005
Threshold	£275,000
(previously £263,000 for transfers after 5 April 2004)	
Death rate	40%

VAT	
Standard rate	17.5%
Registration threshold after 31 March 2005	£60,000
(previously £58,000 after 31 March 2004)	

NATIONAL INSURANCE 2005/06

(2004/05 in brackets where different)

Class 1 Contributions

Not contracted out

The employee contribution is 11% of earnings between £94 (£91) and £630 (£610) p.w. plus 1% of all earnings above £630 (£610) p.w. The employer contribution is 12.8% of all earnings in excess of the first £94 (£91) p.w.

Contracted out

The 'not contracted out' rates for employees are reduced on the band of earnings from £94 (£91) p.w. to £630 (£610) p.w. by 1.6%. For employers, they are reduced on the band of earnings from £94 (£91) p.w. to £630 (£610) p.w. by 3.5% for employees in salary-related schemes or 1.0% for employees in money purchase schemes. In addition, there is an employee rebate of 1.6% and an employer rebate of 3.5% or 1.0%, as appropriate, on earnings from £82 (£79) p.w. up to £94 (£91) p.w.

Class 1A and 1B contributions 12.8%

Class 2 contributions

Flat weekly rate	£2.10	(£2.05)
Exemption limit	£4,345	(£4,215)

Class 3 contributions

Flat weekly rate	£7.35	(£7.15)

Class 4 contributions

8% on the band of profits between £4,895 (£4,745) and £32,760 (£31,720) *plus* 1% on all profits above £32,760 (£31,720).

PERSONAL TAX

Income Tax Rates and Allowances

For 2005/06, the lower, basic and higher rates of income tax remain at 10%, 22% and 40% respectively.

The starting rate band is increased by £70 to £2,090, and the basic rate band by £930 to £30,310 (so that the higher rate applies to taxable income in excess of £32,400).

The special rates applicable to dividends and other savings income are unchanged.

The rate applicable to discretionary and accumulation trusts remains at 40% (32.5% for dividend income). Such trusts will have a new basic rate band of £500.

The basic personal allowance is increased by £150 to £4,895. For this and other personal reliefs, see the table on page 1.

Pensions Schemes Earnings Cap

From 6 April 2005, the maximum level of earnings for which pension provision may be made under tax-approved occupational, personal and stakeholder pension schemes is increased by £3,600 to £105,600.

In addition, the final remuneration cap of £100,000 for occupational schemes approved after 16 March 1987 and before 27 July 1989 is also increased to £105,600. This has the effect of taking the cap on tax-free lump sums from £150,000 to £158,400 (i.e. 1.5 times final remuneration).

Civil Partnerships

The Civil Partnership Act 2004 (CPA) creates an entirely new legal status of civil partner, giving same-sex couples in the United Kingdom the opportunity of acquiring a legal status for their relationship. For tax purposes, the Government has announced that civil partners will be treated the same as married couples. The tax changes will take effect from 5 December 2005.

The most significant changes are as follows:

- Transfers between civil partners in lifetime or on death will generally be exempt from inheritance tax without limit.
- Only one property owned by a couple who are civil partners, whether that property is owned solely or jointly, may be treated as the principal private residence of either of them at any time for the purposes of capital gains tax private residence relief.
- Transfers of assets between persons who are civil partners who are living together will be on a no-gain no-loss basis for capital gains tax purposes.
- Pension tax legislation will be amended so that references to husband, wife, ex-husband, ex-wife, spouse, ex-spouse, surviving spouse, widow, widower will now include civil partner, former civil partner and surviving civil partner under the terms of the CPA.
- There will be an exemption from stamp duty and stamp duty land tax for transactions carried out in connection with the dissolution of a civil partnership so that transfers of shares or the transfer of the partners' home from joint ownership into the sole ownership of one of the ex-partners is exempt.
- Where one of the partners was born before 6 April 1935 the partners will be entitled to an allowance equivalent to the married couple's allowance.
- Anti-avoidance legislation will be extended to include civil partners in the same way as spouses, including the legislation relating to settlements, company control and the transfer of assets abroad.

EMPLOYMENT TAX

Company Car and Fuel Benefit

The figure for calculating car fuel benefit is unchanged for 2005/06 at £14,400.

The CO_2 emissions limits for the minimum petrol percentage car benefit charge for 2005/06 and 2006/07 have been set at 140 g/km and this figure will be frozen for 2007/08.

Discounts for cars that can run on alternative fuels will be simplified for 2006/07 as follows:

- cost of conversion disregarded for bi-fuel and petrol cars converted after type approval; no additional discount;
- 2% for bi-fuel gas and petrol cars manufactured or converted before type approval;
- 3% discount for hybrid electric and petrol cars; and
- 6% for electric-only cars.

Computer and Bicycle Exemptions

The 'benefit in kind' rules will be changed from 6 April 2005, to ensure that no tax charge arises where employees buy computers or bicycles from their employer, provided that the bicycle or computer has previously been loaned to them or to another employee, and that they pay market value. (At present a tax charge may arise under ITEPA 2003, s 206.)

Outplacement Counselling and Training

From 6 April 2005 both part and full-time employees will be able to receive tax-free outplacement counselling and retraining expenses when they lose their job. Currently a tax exemption is only available to employees who work full-time. The proposed revision will also extend the duration of the retraining course covered by the tax exemption from one year to two and removes the condition that the course has to be full-time or substantially full-time.

Payments to Employees in Full-Time Education

The limit for tax-free payments by employers to employees in full-time education at a recognised educational establishment has been increased to £15,000 for an academic year and can also now be paid free of Class 1 NICs.

The revised treatment will apply to payments for the 2005/06 academic year, commencing 1 September 2005.

Statement of Practice 4/86 (SP 4/86) has been updated and the link to payments by public awarding bodies has been removed.

Pension Protection Fund

The Pension Protection Fund (PPF) was set up by Pensions Act 2004. Its purpose is to assume responsibility for final salary occupational pension schemes (and other pension schemes with defined benefit elements) whose sponsoring employers have become insolvent, leaving insufficient assets in the scheme. The PPF will pay compensation to pension scheme members in lieu of the benefits that would have been payable under the scheme.

The PPF will be a body corporate and will be funded by statutory levies on eligible schemes, for which tax relief would not necessarily be given. As it is not itself a pension scheme, the PPF would not be able to pay tax-free lump sums. In order to remove these anomalies, the PPF will be given equivalent tax treatment to that of a Revenue-approved occupational pension scheme for 2005/06 and that of a registered pension scheme for 2006/07 onwards (under the new universal pensions regime due to come into effect on 6 April 2006).

Research Institution Spinout Companies

The regime relating to employment-related securities will be amended so that the value of intellectual property transferred by research institutions to spinout companies is ignored at the time of transfer. This will remove a potential PAYE and NIC charge on the transfer.

The aim of the legislation is to restore the level of activity in setting up spinout companies by removing any uncertainty of tax treatment. It will be effective from 2 December 2004, with an election available for spinout companies set up before that date to defer the charge to income tax and NIC. The deadline for such an election will be 15 October 2005.

Armed Forces Pension and Compensation Payments

Existing legislation will be adjusted so that the tax exemptions under current schemes will apply to payments made under new Armed Forces Pension, Compensation and Early Departure Payments Schemes. Also exempt from income tax are lump sum in-service compensation payments made under the Armed Forces Compensation Scheme.

The new schemes will pay benefits from 6 April 2005, from when the tax exemption also applies.

BUSINESS TAX

Landlord's Energy Saving Allowance

This allowance, introduced in the 2004 Budget, will be extended from 7 April 2005 to capital expenditure by landlords on the installation of solid wall insulation in dwelling houses which they let. The allowance is 100% of the expenditure incurred, up to a maximum of £1,500 per building, and already applies to the installation of loft insulation or cavity wall insulation.

Renovation of Business Premises

A 100% first-year allowance (the 'Business Premises Renovation Allowance' (BPRA)) is to be introduced for capital expenditure incurred by individuals and companies (whether as landlords or tenants) on the renovation or conversion of vacant business premises, in any of the disadvantaged areas of the UK designated as 'Enterprise Areas', for the purpose of bringing those premises back into business use. The scheme will be restricted to property that has been vacant for at least a year. The commencement date is dependent on EU State Aid approval and is as yet undetermined.

Film Tax Relief

Under current rules (F(No 2)A 1997, s 48), production and acquisition expenditure on a low budget (£15 million or less) film certified by the Department for Culture, Media and Sport as a qualifying British film can be fully deducted for tax purposes in the year in which it is incurred, instead of being written off over a longer period. This relief had been due to expire on 1 July 2005 but will now be extended to 31 March 2006. This extension will enable low budget films to qualify for the current relief if the first day of principal photography is no later than 31 March 2006 and the film is completed before 1 January 2007. In the case of acquisition expenditure, it is a further condition that the acquisition of the film must take place before 1 October 2007.

Lloyd's Underwriting Regulations

Amendments are to be made to the powers for making regulations relating to Lloyd's underwriters. This measure amends these regulation-making powers, primarily in order to permit the repeal of FA 1993, Sch 19 and replace it with regulations made by Statutory Instrument. This allows for greater flexibility when amending and modernising the current procedures by, for example, allowing for electronic filing of syndicate returns and by applying self-assessment principles to the determination of syndicate profits. (Lloyd's managing agents are required to make returns to the Inland Revenue of syndicate profits and losses, computed for tax purposes.) This measure will apply to regulations made after the date of Royal Assent.

Landfill Tax

With effect from 1 April 2005, the standard rate of landfill tax is to be increased from £15 per tonne to £18 per tonne. The lower rate of £2 per tonne for inactive waste is to remain unchanged.

From the same date, the maximum credit which landfill site operators may claim against their annual landfill tax liability in respect of contributions to bodies enrolled under the Landfill Tax Credit Scheme is to be reduced from 6.8% to 6%.

From 6 April 2005, the entitlement to exemptions and tax credit which applies to landfill sites where an environmental licence or resolution is in force will be extended to sites where a permit is in force.

CORPORATION TAX

Corporation Tax Rates

The main rate of corporation tax will be set at 30% for financial year 2006. The small companies rate and starting rate are unchanged at 19% and 0% respectively for financial year 2005. The non-corporate distribution rate is also unchanged at 19% for financial year 2005.

Corporate Intangible Assets

Related party rules

For transfers of assets, and debits and credits brought into account, on or after 16 March 2005 the related party rules for corporate intangible assets (in FA 2002, Sch 29) are to be amended to ensure that assets created before 1 April 2002 are excluded from the provisions if they were transferred between 'related parties' on or after that date. The proposed amendment provides for a participator (or a participator's associate) in a close company that controls, or has a major interest in, another close company, to be a related party of that second company. For the purpose of bringing debits and credits into account, the proposed amendments are deemed to be part of the provisions as originally enacted.

Market value rules

For transfers of assets on or after 16 March 2005, the market value rules in FA 2002, Sch 29 are to be amended to prevent related parties gaining a tax advantage by agreeing an artificially high or low price for the asset. Where assets are transferred at an under or over-value, the proposals will ensure that Schedule 29 does not prevent a taxable distribution or employment income from arising. Secondly, where capital gains tax gifts relief is claimed on an asset gifted to a related-party company, the company's acquisition cost for the purposes of Schedule 29 is to be the market value less the amount of the held-over gain.

New class of assets

Payment entitlement under the single payment scheme for farmers will, for acquisitions of payment entitlement on or after 22 March 2005, fall within the rules for corporate intangible assets. Under the proposals, such payments will, therefore, not be eligible as replacement assets for the purposes of capital gains rollover and hold-over relief.

International Accounting Standards (IAS)

A number of technical amendments are proposed to the legislation in FA 2004 and to regulations made in December 2004 to reflect recent developments in accounting practice and also to correct some errors and omissions in the 2004 legislation.

It is further proposed that special purpose vehicle companies (SPVs) in a defined category can, for all accounting periods beginning in 2005, continue to use UK GAAP as it stood on 31 December 2004 for the purpose of computing their taxable profits, even where they make the transition to preparing accounts under IAS or revised UK GAAP. The Finance Bill is also to contain a power to make regulations setting out a permanent scheme of taxation for SPVs.

An anti-avoidance measure is to be introduced to prevent companies crystallising losses in advance of the transition to IAS.

Life Insurance Companies

Measures affecting the taxation of life insurance companies will be included in the Finance Bill. These will affect the following:

- Transfers of business from one life insurance company to another (note that there are significant differences from material published at the time of the pre-Budget report in 2004). This will apply to transfers of business after 1 December 2004.
- The treatment of receipts as 'notional'. This will apply to accounting periods ending after 1 December 2004.
- The use of sub-funds to obtain a more favourable tax apportionment of investment return. This will apply to accounting periods beginning after 31 December 2004.
- The tax treatment of income and gains attributable to assets not needed to pay policyholder benefits. For accounting periods beginning after 31 December 2004 these will be taxed at normal corporation tax rates.

Oil Companies

Corporation tax and supplementary charge payable by oil companies on their ring-fence profits is to be paid by way of three equal instalments, rather than by quarterly instalments as at present. The new rules will apply to the tax liability of companies with ring-fence profits in respect of accounting periods ending after 30 June 2005. For companies with calendar year accounting periods, the first instalment affected will be that due on 14 January 2006. There will be transitional arrangements for the first accounting period ending after 30 June 2005.

CAPITAL GAINS

Temporary Non-Residents

Amendments will be made to close loopholes in the capital gains tax regime governing temporary non-residence (TCGA 1992, s 10A). The law is tightened in two main areas.

- Those who are resident or ordinarily resident in the UK and simultaneously resident for tax treaty purposes in a territory outside the UK ('Treaty non-resident') will be treated as neither resident nor ordinarily resident in the UK (although this will not affect the operation of provisions attributing gains of offshore companies or trusts to UK-based individuals). Without this change the regime is ineffective because the individual never ceases to be resident or ordinarily resident in the UK.
- Where a liability arises in a territory outside the UK under a double taxation agreement, this will not prevent a charge arising on return to the UK (although relief will be available for any foreign tax paid). This prevents an advantage being gained by realising assets in a low-tax jurisdiction.

These provisions will have effect where the tax year of departure (or deemed non-residence under the new legislation) is 2005/06. They will also have effect if the year of departure (or deemed non-residence) is 2004/05 provided there is a time between 16 March and 5 April 2005 when the individual is resident or ordinarily resident in the UK and not simultaneously resident in a territory outside the UK.

The opportunity is taken to make other, more minor, changes to TCGA 1992, s 10A.

Location of Assets

An anti-avoidance measure, which takes effect from 16 March 2005, will mean that certain assets are treated as being located in the UK for capital gains purposes.

The measure is intended to prevent avoidance by individuals who are resident or ordinarily resident, but not domiciled, in the UK and persons carrying on a trade, profession or vocation, via a branch, agency or permanent establishment in the UK though neither resident nor ordinarily resident.

The following specific location rules will apply.

- Registered debentures of a company not incorporated in the UK will be treated as situated where the register is situated and membership rights in a company with no share capital will be treated in the same way.
- Whether intellectual property rights under the law of a territory outside the UK are situated in the UK will be determined in the same way as for equivalent UK intellectual property rights.
- Certain intangible assets will be treated as situated in the UK at all times if subject to UK law at the time of creation.
- Intangible assets that are options or futures not subject to UK law at the time of their creation will be treated as situated in the UK at all times if they can be satisfied by delivery of an asset situated in the UK, or if any part of the underlying subject matter is shares in, or debentures of, a company incorporated in the UK which are yet to be issued.
- The location for capital gains purposes of a person's interest in an asset jointly owned by two or more persons will be determined as if it were wholly owned by that person.

The changes will have a knock-on effect in relation to the provisions of the accrued income scheme which use the capital gains provisions to determine whether securities are located in the UK.

Trustees' Change of Residence

Amendments will be made to the capital gains tax regime for trusts in order to prevent the use of double taxation agreements to reduce UK exposure. The new legislation will apply where trustees are, at different times within the same tax year:

- resident or ordinarily resident in the UK and not also resident for tax treaty purposes in a territory outside the UK (i.e. not Treaty non-resident); and
- resident or ordinarily resident in the UK but Treaty non-resident, or neither resident nor ordinarily resident in the UK.

The effect of the new legislation will be to ensure that any Double Taxation Agreement may not prevent a charge to UK capital gains tax in any year in which the above residence circumstances apply. There will be appropriate credit for any foreign tax suffered.

The new measure applies to disposals of settled property after 15 March 2005.

SAVINGS AND INVESTMENTS

ISA Limits

Individual Savings Account (ISA) limits of £7,000 maximum and £3,000 for cash will be retained until 5 April 2010. (They had been due to fall from 6 April 2006.)

ISAs and Child Trust Funds

The Government will extend the rules for qualifying investments in Individual Savings Accounts (ISAs) and Child Trust Funds (CTFs), allowing the holders of such accounts and funds to invest in all retail collective investment schemes authorised by the Financial Services Authority (FSA).

The extension will take effect from 6 April 2006. It will cover authorised schemes which qualify as 'UCITS' schemes under the European Directive on Undertakings for Collective Investment in Transferable Securities ('the UCITS Directive'), and 'non-UCITS' retail schemes, which have slightly more relaxed rules, allowing access to a wider range of investment products including real property.

However, the schemes must not restrict savers' ability to access their savings and schemes which apply the FSA's 'limited redemption' rule will not be eligible.

Pensions Tax Simplification

Legislation introducing an extensive and universal new regime for personal and occupational pensions was introduced in Finance Act 2004 and is due to come into force on 6 April 2006. A number of further measures will now be added, most of them covered in an Inland Revenue Technical Note published on 16 February 2005, to provide additional flexibility for pension schemes and contributors, to clarify aspects of the new rules, to smooth the transition from current to new regime and to introduce further anti-avoidance and compliance rules. Pre-existing schemes will now have at least until 6 April 2011 to modify their scheme rules.

Collective Investment Schemes

There will be changes to the taxation of collective investment schemes (including authorised unit trusts and authorised open-ended investment companies).

The tax arrangements for authorised trusts that issue multiple classes of units will be clarified. There will be 'non-discrimination rules' similar to those that already exist for open-ended investment companies.

The Finance Bill will include powers to change the relevant regulations in order to counter avoidance; to respond to future Financial Services Authority changes; to change the existing distribution rules; and to permit different tax treatment to be applied to different unit/share holders in funds that are 'qualified investor schemes'. The Revenue will 'consider the case for a purposive anti-avoidance test' for qualified investor schemes. Where an investor owns a substantial portion of a qualified investor scheme, any annual increase in the value of their units/shares will be chargeable as income under self-assessment. Gains that are unrealised at the time the rule starts will be held over and treated as chargeable gains when the units are sold.

The rules determining who can receive interest distributions gross will be aligned with the gross payment rules for bank interest. However, this will not affect the deductibility of such distributions when calculating the income of an authorised investment fund chargeable to corporation tax.

Regulations will be drafted to deal with the tax treatment of authorised investment funds that own property, once the government has 'finalised its position' with regard to UK real estate investment trusts.

There are several other minor changes to the relevant provisions.

INHERITANCE TAX

Inheritance Tax Threshold

The inheritance tax nil-rate band for 2005/06 is increased to £275,000. The nil-rate band for future years has been set at £285,000 for 2006/07 and £300,000 for 2007/08.

CHARITIES

Gift Aid and Admissions

Currently, certain heritage and conservation charities may offer free admission in return for a donation without the admission counting as a benefit for Gift Aid purposes. This exemption is to be extended from 6 April 2006 to any type of charity that grants the right to pay to view its property.

However, if a donation is made instead of paying an admission charge, Gift Aid will only apply to the whole of the gift if:

- the right of admission is for an unrestricted number of visits over a period of at least one year; or

- the right of admission is for less than one year but the gift is at least 10% more than the amount any member of the public would have to pay for the same right of admission. If there is not a comparable admission ticket, the value of the right of admission will count towards the benefit limit for Gift Aid purposes (25% of the donation, up to a maximum of £250 in any year).

The effect is that, for admissions after 5 April 2006, charities will no longer be able simply to reclassify admission fees as donations subject to Gift Aid.

TRUSTS

Modernising the Tax System for Trusts

As previewed in last year's Budget, a basic rate band will be introduced and will apply to the first £500 of income of all discretionary trusts and accumulation trusts liable at the 'rate applicable to trusts', which remains at 40% (32.5% for dividend income). The band will apply for 2005/06 onwards. Trusts with total income within the basic rate band will have no further liability on income received net of tax or with accompanying tax credit and will be liable at only basic rate or lower rate (depending on the type of income) on income received gross.

Again as announced last year, a new regime is being introduced for certain trusts with vulnerable beneficiaries. Its introduction is being backdated to 6 April 2004. According to the announcement made last year, the regime will enable such trusts to be taxed on the basis of the vulnerable beneficiary's individual circumstances, taking account of his own personal reliefs and tax rates.

Other measures announced in the 2004 Budget relating to the modernisation of trusts have now been postponed until 6 April 2006 at the earliest. A discussion paper has been published today.

ANTI-AVOIDANCE

Double Tax Relief

Relief for trade receipts

Legislation is to be introduced to deny excessive relief and clarify the law on the restriction for credit relief for foreign tax paid on income taxed in the UK as a trading receipt (such as interest and dividends received by financial traders and rental income from foreign properties). The proposed legislation will clarify which expenses and related transactions should be taken into account in determining the proportion of the net profit or loss attributable to the activity that gave rise to the foreign tax so that the credit for foreign tax paid is restricted to the UK tax on the profits (if any). The rules will apply from 16 March 2005 for companies and from 6 April 2005 for individuals. A transitional rule will apply, from 16 March 2005 to 31 December 2005, to relief for tax withheld from dividends so as not to deny relief for more than half of the foreign tax paid.

Anti-avoidance measures

The following three proposals to restrict double tax relief are to have effect from 16 March 2005.

- Where relief is claimed for foreign tax as part of a scheme or arrangement of which the main purpose (or one of the main purposes) is the avoidance of tax, the relief for double tax is to be limited so as to cancel the scheme or arrangement where it falls within one of five prescribed circumstances. For example, relief will be restricted where the foreign tax credit reduces the tax payable to less than the amount that would have been due had the transaction not occurred. The proposed provisions also apply to underlying tax where the legislation would have applied to the foreign company which paid the tax had that company been resident in the UK and made a claim for relief. The legislation will only apply where the total credit claimed in any one year is not minimal and the Revenue issue a notice to direct that it does. The taxpayer must then decide how the legislation applies and self-assess (or amend an existing self-assessment) as appropriate. The usual self-assessment enquiry and appeal procedures will apply and 'discovery' notices can be issued in certain circumstances.

- Where the provision which taxes a group of companies as a single entity (TA 1988, s 803A) applies, legislation is proposed to limit its scope so that it does not apply to a controlled foreign company for which exemption is available under the acceptable distribution test.
- Credit relief is to be denied for underlying tax in respect of income which is treated as a dividend in the UK but for which a tax deduction has been given in the foreign jurisdiction (where, for example, the payment has been characterised as interest).

Countering Film Tax Avoidance

As highlighted in the Pre-Budget Report, anti-avoidance measures are being introduced as follows to counter tax-avoidance schemes aimed at those producing or investing in films.

- From 2 December 2004 (unless the film was already in production at that date), only one person will be able to claim relief (under F(No 2)A 1992, s 42 or F(No 2)A 1997, s 48) for a qualifying British film, either for production expenditure or acquisition expenditure but not both.
- From 2 December 2004 (unless he has already entered into an unconditional agreement at that date), if a person claims film reliefs and enters into an agreement guaranteeing him income from the exploitation of the film, the reliefs will be restricted to the extent, if any, that guaranteed income will arise more than 15 years after the making of the agreement.
- To prevent groups of companies using 'exit schemes' intended to convert the deferral of tax via film reliefs into permanent avoidance of tax, companies will be required, where the disposal of film rights out of the group occurs on or after 2 December 2004, to treat the value of film rights (so far as not already taxed) as a trading receipt at the time of the exit event.
- To the extent that film reliefs for members of partnerships are already limited by reference to partners' capital contributions to the firm, the rules are being tightened to disregard, from 2 December 2004, any capital contributed which is not genuinely at risk.

In addition, for films starting principal photography on or after 2 December 2004, the rules for low-budget films (F(No 2)A 1997, s 48) will be aligned more closely with those for larger budget films (F(No 2)A 1992, s 42). This will ensure that relief is always restricted to expenditure that is incurred before the film is completed and is payable no later than four months after completion.

Avoidance through Arbitrage

Tax avoidance measures will be introduced to counter arbitrage schemes that involve hybrid entities or hybrid instruments. Such schemes use the differences between national tax codes to produce tax advantages such as a double deduction for the same expense, or a UK deduction for the payer in circumstances where the recipient is not taxed on the receipt. The legislation will only apply where the Revenue gives a notice to that effect. On receipt of a notice, a company must make or amend its self-assessment taking the legislation into account.

The legislation will have different triggering conditions which will result in a Revenue notice being issued: one set applying to claims for a deduction; another set where an amount is received that is not, apart from this new legislation, taxable. The legislation will apply to deductions and receipts arising or accruing on or after 16 March 2005. However, provided connected persons are not involved, it will not apply to schemes involving deductions that are in place on or before 16 March 2005 if they are terminated by 1 July 2005.

The Revenue indicate that they will give assistance on the application of the new legislation to specific cases under Code of Practice 10 procedures. Draft guidance on the general application of the legislation is available on the Revenue website.

Financial Avoidance

Various income tax or corporation tax avoidance schemes involving financial products are to be blocked. Strips of corporate bonds will be brought within the relevant discounted securities regime. Companies' profits from debt securities acquired by way of stock loans or 'repo' agreements will be fully taxable. The company loss-buying rules are to be strengthened for non-trading loan relationship losses.

Generation of artificial capital losses by companies using capital redemption bonds will be prevented by amending the loan relationships rules. Various changes in the loan relationships and derivative contracts rules will prevent companies from converting interest-like income into a capital gain or a 'tax nothing' by using shares or derivatives over shares. A de-grouping charge will apply under the loan relationships and derivative contracts rules, and other group provisions are to be amended. The 15-year exception limit for rent factoring schemes is to be abolished. With minor exceptions, companies' annuities and annual payments will no longer be charges on income, deductibility instead depending on the management expenses regime. Any possibility of a double deduction under the manufactured interest and accrued income scheme rules in respect of an income tax scheme involving a stock loan of gilts is to be eliminated.

STAMP TAXES

Residential Property Threshold

The threshold for stamp duty land tax on residential property has been raised from £60,000 to £120,000. As a result of this change, stamp duty land tax will not be charged on transactions in residential property if the consideration does not exceed £120,000. Where the consideration exceeds £120,000 but does not exceed £250,000, the 1% charge continues to apply. The change in threshold applies to transactions the effective date of which is on or after 17 March 2005. There is, however, no change to the £150,000 threshold for residential transactions in designated disadvantaged areas. When the stamp duty land tax regime came into effect on 1 December 2003, some contracts relating to land transactions remained within the old stamp duty regime. Where such a contract relates to a transaction in residential property, the stamp duty threshold is also raised to £120,000.

Disclosure Rules

FA 2004, ss 307–319 contain provision for the disclosure of tax avoidance schemes in relation to direct taxes. Those sections set out the general rules under which certain promoters and users of tax avoidance schemes must notify the Revenue about the schemes. Current regulations narrow the scope of the existing disclosure requirements to schemes and arrangements involving employment or the use of financial products where the tax advantage concerns income tax, corporation tax or capital gains tax. New regulations are to be made which will address schemes and arrangements involving stamp duty land tax. Promoters (or users, in prescribed circumstances) will be required to inform the Revenue of any schemes or arrangements intended to avoid stamp duty land tax on commercial property transactions. However, this is restricted to cases where the property has a market value of at least £5 million. The rules will apply to schemes or arrangements made available or implemented on or after 1 July 2005.

Commercial Disadvantaged Areas Relief

The stamp duty land tax relief for property in designated disadvantaged areas has been withdrawn for non-residential land transactions. The relief will no longer be available for transactions with an effective date after 16 March 2005. However, where a contract was entered into before that date, and completion or substantial performance occurs after that date, the relief will still be available. This is on condition that there is no variation or assignment of the contract, or sub-sale of the property, and that the transaction is not the exercise of an option or right of pre-emption. Disadvantaged areas relief is still available for residential transactions.

Anti-Avoidance

A series of measures to counter stamp duty land tax avoidance have been announced. These measures block certain schemes involving:

- the use of group relief;
- the use of acquisition relief;
- grants of leases by bare trustees to their principal;
- certain variations of leases to remove restrictive covenants;
- the use of repayable loans or deposits as consideration;
- the reduction of market value by encumbrance;
- the use of sub-sale relief in alternative finance transactions; and
- the use of partnerships.

The measures apply to all land transactions with an effective date on or after 17 March 2005. However, subject to certain conditions, they do *not* apply where a transaction is effected on or after that date in pursuance of a contract entered into before that date. The conditions that must be met are that:

- there is no variation of or assignment of rights under the contract after 16 March 2005;
- the transaction is not effected in consequence of the exercise after 16 March 2005 of any option, right of pre-emption, or similar right; and
- after 16 March 2005, there is no assignment, sub-sale or similar transaction in respect of all or part of the subject-matter, as a result of which a person other than the contracting purchaser becomes entitled to call for a conveyance.

Alternative Finance Arrangements

Changes from 6 April 2005 will ensure that certain finance arrangements which replicate the effects of investments or loans at interest are taxed neither more nor less favourably than equivalent arrangements giving rise to interest. From Royal Assent, changes to the stamp duty land tax (SDLT) regime will extend reliefs to a wider range of alternative property finance arrangements. These changes are designed to facilitate the use of alternative financial products, including those designed to be Shari'a compliant.

Demutualisation of Insurance Companies

Changes are due to be made to the rules on stamp duty and stamp duty reserve tax relief on the demutualisation of insurance companies. Relief is currently available when a mutually owned insurance company restructures and moves its investments to a new company on demutualisation. The new rules will ensure that the transfer of investments in collective investment schemes from the mutual to the new company continues to qualify for relief. The measure will apply from Royal Assent to the Finance Bill.

Reliefs for Multilateral Trading Facilities

Changes are to be made to the scope of the stamp duty and stamp duty reserve tax reliefs for intermediaries and repurchase/stock lending. The reliefs will be extended to members of specified Multilateral Trading Facilities (MTFs) as defined by the EU Markets in Financial Instruments Directive 2004/39/EC. This will enable the Treasury to designate specified MTFs as being, in effect, a 'recognised exchange' for the purposes of the reliefs. The change will take effect from Royal Assent to the Finance Bill.

VALUE ADDED TAX

Registration and Deregistration

With effect from 1 April 2005, the VAT registration threshold (the annual taxable turnover limit which determines whether a person must be registered for VAT) will be increased from £58,000 to £60,000. The deregistration threshold will be increased from £56,000 to £58,000. The registration and deregistration thresholds for acquisitions from other EU member states will also be increased from £58,000 to £60,000.

Car Fuel Scale Charges

The scale used to charge VAT on fuel used for private motoring in business cars will be increased from the start of the first VAT period beginning on or after 1 May 2005. The revised scale charges are as follows:

Annual returns

Cylinder capacity of vehicle	Scale charge diesel	VAT due per car	Scale charge petrol	VAT due per car
	£	£	£	£
Up to 1,400 cc	945	140.74	985	146.70
1,401 cc to 2,000 cc	945	140.74	1,245	185.43
2,001 cc or more	1,200	178.72	1,830	272.55

Quarterly returns

Cylinder capacity of vehicle	Scale charge diesel	VAT due per car	Scale charge petrol	VAT due per car
	£	£	£	£
Up to 1,400 cc	236	35.15	246	36.64
1,401 cc to 2,000 cc	236	35.15	311	46.32
2,001 cc or more	300	44.68	457	68.06

Monthly returns

Cylinder capacity of vehicle	Scale charge diesel	VAT due per car	Scale charge petrol	VAT due per car
	£	£	£	£
Up to 1,400 cc	78	11.62	82	12.21
1,401 cc to 2,000 cc	78	11.62	103	15.34
2,001 cc or more	100	14.89	152	22.64

The Commissioners are consulting with businesses on a proposal to change the basis of the scale charge from one based on engine size and fuel type to one based on CO_2 emissions. The purpose is to align the Customs and Revenue scale charge systems and to provide tax incentives in line with the Government's environmental objectives.

Reduced Rate for Charities

The reduced rate of 5% is to apply to supplies of advice or information relating to the welfare of the elderly or disabled, and children. The relief will apply, for example, to child protection videos or expert advice on the welfare of children or the elderly when provided by charities working in those areas.

Goods and services which are currently exempt are unaffected by the change.

The operative date of the change is subject to consultation.

Reduced Rate for Air Source Heat Pumps

With effect from 7 April 2005, air source heat pumps and micro combined heat and power units will be subject to the 5% reduced rate of VAT.

Local Authorities — Reclassification of Services

With effect from 1 April 2005, certain services of a social nature (including childcare and welfare) provided by local authorities are to be regarded as non-business. Such services are currently regarded as exempt business activities, giving rise to a restriction of the VAT recoverable on related costs. The change will allow such VAT to be recovered under the provisions of VATA 1994, s 33.

The precise scope of the services covered by the change has yet to be announced, but only those services which are of a social nature and which local authorities have a special duty to provide will be covered.

Avoidance Scheme Disclosure Rules

With effect from Royal Assent, businesses will be required to disclose when they use or are party to schemes that give a tax advantage that does not appear on their VAT returns, for example in relation to VAT that cannot be deducted because it relates to exempt supplies or non-business activity.

In addition, businesses will be required to disclose when they use schemes that exploit differences between the UK and another EU member state's treatment of vouchers; and that attempt to remove the effect of an election to waive exemption on supplies of land and property.

A new 'hallmark' of avoidance is also being introduced, to require disclosure of schemes that make use of face value vouchers with low redemption rates.

Partial Exemption

With effect from 1 April 2005, there will be four changes to the VAT Regulations governing partial exemption.

The first change will extend Customs' policy on the use of their existing power to serve a special method override notice. Customs will serve a notice in any circumstances where they have clear evidence that the current special method is not fair and there is a significant loss of revenue.

Secondly, there will be a requirement that in future, approval or direction of a partial exemption special method must be in writing.

Thirdly, where a special method makes no provision for how to deal with certain types of input tax, that input tax will be recovered to the extent that the goods or services on which it has been incurred are actually used in making taxable supplies.

Fourthly, the benefit of 'rounding' will only be available to businesses whose 'residual' input tax is less than £400,000 per month. Customs will no longer approve rounding up in special methods.

Overpayments — Unjust Enrichment

With effect from 23 March 2005, the rules regarding unjust enrichment will no longer be limited to claims where VAT has been overpaid; they will apply to any case where output tax has been overcharged, even if the amount in question was not actually paid (e.g. because the relevant return gave rise to a net repayment).

The three-year cap will continue to apply to all claims of overpayment. However, the three-year period will commence as follows:

- where the error has been made on a return, from the end of the period covered by the return;
- where the error has been made on a voluntary disclosure, from the end of the period in which the disclosure is made;
- where the error has been accounted for in an assessment, from the end of the period in which the assessment is made;
- where the error arises as a result of a duplicate payment, from the date of the overpayment.

Supplies of Goods in Customs' Warehouses

Under EU law, supplies of goods in customs warehouses are disregarded for VAT purposes provided that the amount of VAT which would have been due corresponds to the amount due on removal from warehouse. Exploitation of the UK legislation (VATA 1994, s 18) has meant that this condition is not always met.

Consequently, with effect from a date following Royal Assent, the Commissioners will be able to disapply the provisions of VATA 1994, s 18(1) in cases of abuse.

Supplies of Gas and Electricity from Abroad

With effect from 17 March 2005, the value, for VAT purposes, of supplies of gas and electricity received by taxable persons from suppliers established abroad is the consideration payable to the supplier. (Taxable persons have been required to account for VAT on such supplies since 1 January 2005, but until this announcement the value of the supply had not been established.)

TAXES ON EXPENDITURE

Alcohol Duty

The excise duty on spirits, cider and sparkling wine is frozen. The duty on beer and still wine is increased by 2.6%, adding 1p to a pint of beer and 1p to a standard 175ml glass of wine.

Tobacco Products

The rates of duty on tobacco products imported into, or manufactured in, the UK are increased by 2.6% (in line with inflation).

Gaming Duty

The Gross Gaming Yield threshold for each duty band will be increased in line with inflation, for accounting periods starting on or after 1 April 2005.

The new duty bands are as shown below:

First £534,500	2.5%
Next £1,186,500	12.5%
Next £1,186,500	20%
Next £2,078,000	30%
Remainder	40%

Hydrocarbon Oils

With effect from 1 September 2005, excise duty rates on main road fuels will be increased by 1.22p per litre in line with inflation. All other hydrocarbon oils for road fuel will also increase in line with inflation. Effective rates of duty for non-road fuels will also be increased by 1.22p per litre. In order to maintain the current differentials with main road fuels, the duty rates for biodiesel, bioethanol and natural gas will also be increased by 1.22p per litre. In the case of road fuel gas other than natural gas (e.g. liquefied petroleum gas), the duty differential will be narrowed by the equivalent of 1p per litre.